We Will Feast

We Will Feast

Rethinking Dinner, Worship, and the Community of God

Kendall Vanderslice

WILLIAM B. EERDMANS PUBLISHING COMPANY
GRAND RAPIDS, MICHIGAN

Wm. B. Eerdmans Publishing Co.
4035 Park East Court SE, Grand Rapids, Michigan 49546
www.eerdmans.com

Published 2019
Printed in the United States of America

25 24 23 22 21 20 19   1 2 3 4 5 6 7

ISBN 978-0-8028-7630-0

Library of Congress Cataloging-in-Publication Data

A catalog record for this book is available from the Library of
Congress.

To the women of Chez Heureuse:
who taught me the joy of intentional living,
whether laughing together around the dinner table,
crying on the kitchen floor, or filling our home with as
many friends as the living room could hold

Contents

CONTENTS

Foreword

Some of the best meals I have ever eaten have been the most surprising. The meal in a village of India, where a family fasted in order to feed me, their guest. The fry bread with blueberry sauce made by an elderly woman in my apartment complex. The fluffy cinnamon roll made by the ex–gang member, tattoos running down his face. The meals cooked by refugee friends from Syria, Afghanistan, Somalia, Cuba, Libya, Myanmar, Nepal. The church potluck where everyone showed up with a bag of chips and nothing more.

Eating with others changes a person—at least I know it has changed me. As a good Christian girl and then as an aspiring activist, I have always struggled with wanting to save the world and with being overcome by the cares of the world as a result. And I don't think it is a stretch to say that meals have saved my soul. Feasting together with people who have suffered on earth has restored my faith in a God of abundance, even when circumstances point in another direction. Eating with others taps into both an elemental need for survival and the holy joy of celebration at the exact same time. A meal savored with other glorious image-bearers does not save the world, but it helps restore our hearts in order to keep moving through it.

In her book *We Will Feast*, Kendall Vanderslice reveals to the reader the fresh wind of the Holy Spirit at work in our churches, homes, and communities. Chapter after chapter I was amazed at the creative, unsung, simple, and profound ways in which people who have been transformed by Christ are living out their faith. These are not the kinds of Christians who get big book deals or are speaking on conference circuits, but these are the faithful people through whom the kingdom of God is coming in our midst.

I think now is a profound time to consider the implications of what Christian community can look like in a deeply divided and unequal society. Vanderslice continually brings the reader back to Jesus, who conducted most of his ministry at a dinner table, who feasted primarily with the poor and the outcast. Jesus also lived in a time of great injustice, perhaps exemplified by the overwhelming number of people who experienced food scarcity during his time, with many individuals not knowing where their next meal would come from. And yet, Vanderslice says, in this context Jesus feasted constantly. When he turned water into wine, he made a lot—

and of the best quality possible! When he fed the five thousand, he made sure there were baskets and baskets overflowing with extra bread and fish.

These stories, and the stories of believers who have tried to model this kind of hospitality, will continue to grow in importance in our own age of abundance, excess, and growing inequality. Food, and our relationship to it, brings up so many issues: broken systems, economic exploitation of the poor, power dynamics, and our own tendency toward insular thinking and homogeneity. But what happens when we make a conscious decision to break out of these ways of living and thinking? Something holy happens.

This isn't a typical book on how to be more hospitable—how to create a cozy, comfortable environment, one filled with simple recipes that will impress your guests. Instead, *We Will Feast* is a meditation on true neighborliness, rooted in the reality of both the New Testament context and the current American Protestant church. It flips the narrative, focusing on how Jesus was dependent on the hospitality of others. And it looks at how Christians are starting to see that they need their neighbors—especially those who are different from them—in order to experience true communion, in order to start being consumed by Jesus Christ himself. People can, and are, learning to grow in the love of an abundant provider-God and to keep their eyes open for those who could always be added to the feast at hand. "Holy food for holy people," as one pastor in these pages says.

As a white evangelical, I'm struck by how I was raised to believe Jesus came to save my soul, which in practice meant my mind. But this book reminds me that Jesus also came to feed my actual body. It is so much simpler and more elemental than I could possibly realize. I am seeing food in light of our global reality, of cultures, of scarcity. I am thinking about food as it relates not just to me but to my neighbors. In her epilogue, Vanderslice writes that "worship around the table is a communal search for every glimmer of goodness in an aching world." It instantly brought me back to some of my most treasured meals, always eaten with neighbors from far and wide.

This book ostensibly chronicles the various forms of dinner churches that are on the rise in America. But truly it is a book about the wider work of the Holy Spirit and a church that is creatively finding small ways of renewal in some of the most unlikely spaces. No matter what your relationship to or definition of church might be, there is space in this book to catch a glimpse of the joy, abundance, and holy imagination of what it means to feast together in this world that we call the House of the Lord. It will surprise you, just like the very best meals always do.

D. L. MAYFIELD
January 2019

Introduction

In 2008, Brooklyn pastor Emily Scott announced that her church, Saint Lydia's, would begin holding their weekly service over dinner. Longing to dispel feelings of isolation that city living fosters for so many young New Yorkers, Scott decided to model her service around the early church practice of Eucharist, having a meal together.

From those beginnings and in the span of just a few years, small, independent dinner-church communities emerged all around the world. These communities do not focus on worship first and then eating together later; they understand the *meal itself* as worship. These churches encompass a range of denominations, both conservative and progressive. Found in urban, suburban, and rural areas, they attract wealthy, middle-class, and unhoused neighbors. The congregations are intergenerational and multiethnic—reflecting the demographics of their particular locations. Some meet in restaurants, others in gardens and on farms, a few in church basements, and the rest wherever they can find the space. Services aren't limited to Sundays: across the country, a dinner-church service takes place every night of the week. What these fellowships all hold in common is a firm belief that Christian worship at the Communion table is much more than a taste of bread and wine.

This form of worship is nothing new. After all, the gospel is a story of meals, opening in a garden and ending at a feast. Records of the early church suggest that they primarily met for worship through eating meals. But over the last thousand years, many churches have lost focus on the centrality of food—and with it a powerful method for the unification of Christ's diverse body. As worshipping communities transition from sanctuaries to farmland and from pews to tables, their demographics shift too. Across the country, a range of denominations boasts of dinner-church congregations diverse in age, race, marital status, income level, and sexual orientation. Men and women nervous to step through the doors of a sanctuary, hesitant to sit next to one another in a pew, are finding God together as they dig through dirt and feast on bread.

The narrative arc of the gospel—from creation and its fall, to Christ's death and resurrection, to the building anticipation of a restored earth—is grounded in the act of eating. Meals end in death and meals offer new life.

The book of Genesis opens in a garden, where humanity receives her primary responsibility: to care for and tend the earth. The only restriction placed on those first humans was a restriction on what they could eat. God said to feast upon fruits from all the trees, so long as they stayed away from just the tree of knowledge of good and evil. The temptation proved too great. In feasting on the forbidden fruit, the man and woman faced a sinister kind of death: every relationship God designed as good—relationships with the soil, with fleshly bodies, with one another—now brought a dimension of evil.

But in God's love for the beloved creation God called it good, and in the narrative that continues through Jesus, humanity received a ministry of meals. Here, Jesus reconciled the relationships that were broken by the knowledge of evil. Reclaiming the cross from a sign of death to a gift and symbol of the continuation of life, Jesus asked his followers to do one thing: to eat. Through consuming bread and wine, Jesus gave his followers a way to again honor the interconnectedness of all of creation. Feasting together, they remembered him and his promises of a coming Kingdom, an eternal banquet in the presence of God, and an end to death and pain and evil.

This contemporary revival of the early church practice of shared meals as Eucharist and worship suggests something important. As our world devalues interpersonal contact in preference for digital media, as differences in belief create deep fractures in denominations, and as the political landscape continues to reinforce division, people long to sit down together and eat, to share a physical communion of together remembering Christ at the table.

Something powerful happens at the table.

I attended my first dinner-church worship service on a warm Thursday evening. Working on a master of liberal arts in gastronomy, I'd recently designed a research project studying the formation of friendships over a series of meals, and I had a personal interest in theology and food, but I did not yet see a connection between the two. The Eucharist compelled me to believe that food could somehow serve as a tool for community-building and peacemaking. That summer I'd been questioning whether to leave my food studies program and turn to seminary when two friends asked me to ride with them out to central Massachusetts to attend Simple Church.

When we pulled into the idyllic New England town square—four churches, a library, and a strip of small businesses situated around a large green and gazebo—I felt as though I'd driven into the set of my favorite TV show. Turning toward the parking lot of the Congregational church, we watched children toss a Frisbee and a young, bearded man dressed in red plaid and a black beanie greet the stream of women and men walking through the door. An older woman carried her casserole dish of mac and cheese. A father arrived with his four ravenous sons. A farmer and his veterinarian wife bore a salad of fresh vegetables.

"Hi, I'm Pastor Zach!" The bearded man introduced himself in his thick Texan drawl. He embraced my two friends in a big hug; they knew one another from seminary. "I'm so glad y'all drove all the way out here!"

As Pastor Zach transitioned from his post at the door to the church basement, he strummed his guitar and began singing, "This little light of mine, I'm gonna let it shine. Jesus gave it to me, I'm gonna let it shine." The children scrambled to the center of the room to dance while the twenty or so adults formed a circle around the perimeter of the space. After the song, we prayed together before Pastor Zach delivered the first half of the Communion liturgy.

"We gather on a Thursday night to eat. On another Thursday night, a long time ago, a group of friends gathered at a table together. And at that dinner, Jesus took the bread and he lifted it up and gave thanks. He broke it and gave it to his friends, saying, 'Eat this in remembrance of me.'" After eating a handful of freshly baked bread, torn from a loaf passed around the circle from neighbor to neighbor, we walked through a buffet of soup, salad, pasta, and more bread, filling plates high before finding seats at a table. We sipped our soup while listening to the day's lectionary reading and hearing a short sermon. And then we talked.

"You don't have to agree with your neighbors," Zach advised the group as we transitioned into a time of discussion. "In fact, it's great if you don't! Listen to what they have to say, ask questions, and understand why you disagree." I sat at a table with a single, evangelical father, a lesbian couple—both mainline Protestant ministers—and a young woman who called herself spiritual but not religious. As we moved through three discussion prompts written on a chalkboard by the buffet, we clearly did disagree. While we all held firmly to our varying beliefs, our surety pushed us toward lively debate rather than argument or frustration. We closed by worshipping in song together and drinking a generous pour of grape juice—reminding ourselves that while we disagree we still come together to worship God.

As my friends and I drove away from the surreal little town that night, the lights of the gazebo flickering in the distance, my mind buzzed. While I'd taken Communion for most of my life, this was the first time I'd actually experienced it. It was transformative.

Over the coming weeks I ruminated on the evening, seeking to understand the experience in light of my research on food and friendship. From that point, in less than a month's time, I drew up a research plan, consulted with my school's internal review board, partnered with a sociologist at the university's School of Theology, and launched into my food studies thesis.

I began to study the Simple Church community, joining them in worship and interviewing congregants about their experiences. As a researcher I was supposed to maintain a reflective approach, remaining one step removed and aware of the ways my very presence affected my findings. But I found *myself* transformed every week as I dined. As my research came to a close, the congregation embraced me as one of their own, pulling me along on their journey to discover how to be the church together. By the time I'd finished writing my thesis, they presented me with an official offer of employment. For a year and a half, I spent my Thursday evenings sitting at the children's table, engaging the church's youngest members in mealtime conversation; the rest of the week I ran the church's bread bakery, making bread and selling it at farmers' markets both as ministry and monastic-style funding.

But the researcher in me never let go. Fascinated by the worldwide movement of dinner churches, I continued independent research on the breadth of meal-centered communities. I encountered an interdenominational network of pastors encouraging one another as they explore new ways of doing church. Every time I hear pastors speak in excitement about the work they are doing, I grow further convinced that this movement is the Holy Spirit engaged in reconciling work.

A shared hunger for an embodiment of the Lord's Supper has fostered dialogue among dinner-church pastors from a range of denominations living in the United States, Canada, and Europe. The intergenerational tables they set encourage discussions among men, women, and children with a wide variety of life experiences. In dining together, these congregations embody the very purpose and work of the church. When Jesus commanded followers to eat together in remembrance of him, he meant it. He knew that eating together would re-member and heal the divisions of the broken body made one in Christ.

In order to overcome the differences that threaten the unity of Christ's body, writes social psychologist Christena Cleveland, we must cling to an identity that is more encompassing than our identities of difference.[1] It can be difficult to cling first and foremost to the identity of Christ-follower when the identity of conservative, progressive, liturgical, evangelical, Baptist, or Anglican keeps us from listening to other followers of the same Christ. But the identity of dinner-church pastor serves as a powerful intermediary—unifying pastors who embody a range of differing beliefs in the remembrance that Christ is present at the table. Simultaneously the tables they set foster dialogue among church members often stifled by differences in belief.

Methodist bishop Larry Goodpaster writes that despite the many varying opinions about how the sacrament should be served and what it means, "there is a common sense that something holy, something transformational, something grace-filled happens" at the table. "As a result," he says, "the Eucharist may indeed provide a way forward and a way for this divided, suspicious world to find its way to a different place, an alternative and holy vision of what it means to be in community."[2] I am beginning to understand there is no better platform for the Eucharist to do such reconciling work than when eaten in the context of a full meal.

The dinner-church model is not perfect; every pastor is open about the difficulties she or he has faced. Whether reconciling with a denomination that practices a closed table (a theology that understands the Eucharist as reserved for baptized believers), or funding a meal for a church with mostly low-income members, to questioning whether one church can ever be truly welcoming to *all*, these pastors must decipher how to make this model work within the limitations of their own denominations and locations. The beauty of meal-centered worship, though, is its adaptability to so many different contexts.

By turning the process of eating into an act of worship, each church is perfectly poised to identify the physical needs in their communities and use their worship to address those needs.

In the following pages of this book, as you read the stories of each church, my hope is that you too will see God at work in all of these meals and begin to encounter God every time you sit down at a table to eat.

1

On Delight

The Gospel as a Story of Meals

When I was sixteen, I would knead through my emotions late into the night, calmed by the manipulation of dough in the silence of my parents' kitchen. I dreamed then of going to culinary school to study baking and pastry. By the time I was in college, whenever I wasn't doing homework, I was scooping cupcakes and shaping cinnamon rolls—leaving my campus apartment in the early hours of the morning and running to class dusted with flour and powdered sugar.

I found ways to weave my interest in food into each class and quickly discovered that anthropology of food was a field of study. As my gastronomic interests developed, I began to read the Bible in new ways, too. For the first time in my life, I deeply craved the bread and wine shared every Sunday morning. As I grew increasingly convinced that God cares about food, I also became convinced that a theological view of food could be key to understanding the interplay of health, good flavor, and environmental sustainability.

In the final week of school I shared with my classmates the beautiful parallels I'd begun to see, starting from the opening pages of Scripture.

The book of Genesis says that God created the heavens and the earth—the Great Gardener crafted life out of nothing. After separating light and dark, earth and sky, God formed physical matter beginning with soil: *Adamah* in Hebrew is the dry ground out of which sprung trees, and plants, and seed-bearing fruits that could carry on the cycle of life. God filled the earth and the seas with all kinds of creatures, big and small, and called all of it good.

Then God said, "Let's craft one more thing, a creature in our image." Picking up a handful of the lush *adamah*, God breathed into it the breath of life, creating the *adam*, Hebrew for human being. God called this creation very good.

The world functioned in beautiful interdependence. The seed-bearing fruit, the animals, and the humans filled the earth with new life. God told the human beings to attend to only one task: govern the earth out of which they were made, resting in the mutual reliance among humans, animals, and soil.

Two trees stood together in the middle of the garden where these first humans lived—the tree of life and the tree of knowledge of good and evil. Just as God had given the humans only one responsibility, God gave them only one restriction as well—a restriction on what they could eat. God told them, "Feast upon the fruits of all of the trees, but stay away from one: the tree of knowledge of good and evil." When temptation proved too great, they plucked from the forbidden tree and they ate. They took the vegetation intended to sustain and be sustained by them, and they used it to fulfill their own selfish desires.

Immediately their eyes were opened. They realized that everything God created and called good could be wielded for evil as well. In just one quick meal, all the relationships that God designed as good—relationships with their bodies, with the ground, with one another, and ultimately with God—became relationships covered in shame. Their selfish desires disrupted the delicate interdependence that allowed for the flourishing of all creation.

With juice still dripping down her fingers, the woman looked at her naked body. Rather than behold the beauty of her curves or the powerful ability for her belly to bring forth new life, she saw the dimples of her thighs and the softness of her middle. The man felt sweat break out upon his brow as the soil sprouted forth thorns and thistles. They felt shame at the nakedness they'd always known as beauty, and they looked to the vegetation around to cover up.

With the cycle of flourishing broken apart, the joy of new life—whether out of the ground or out of the woman's body—required sweat, and tears, and pain. Even the soil itself could not bring forth new life without making compost of death. God banished humanity from the garden and yet never abandoned creation— the material manifestation of the Creator's overflowing love.

God looked tenderly on a woman named Mary and breathed into her belly the breath of life—and behold, a new *adam*. Jesus became the embodiment of God as man, taking on sweat, tears, and pain. Jesus lived his life on earth through a ministry of meals: dining with society's most marginalized; turning water into the finest wine and five loaves and two fish into a meal for a crowd of thousands; extending forgiveness to Peter in an offering of fish; making himself known through the breaking of bread with his disciples on the path to Emmaus.

One small meal had brought death into the world, and through death Jesus reclaimed the meal as a sign of the continuation of life. "As you feast together," he told his followers, "don't dwell on the meal that brought with it death. Feast and remember this bread and this wine, my body and my blood, this death that brings the world back to life."

Remember the interconnectedness of all of creation. Remember God's desire for this beloved world to flourish altogether. And remember that, soon, the Triune God will restore creation once again, and there will be no more death and no more mourning.

In the closing scenes of Revelation, the garden reappears. Only one tree stands in the center, the tree of life—a tree whose leaves can heal nations and that bears its fruit all year round. The option of evil is no longer found. The curse brought on by the *adam*'s fateful bite is reversed and interdependence is restored. The *adam* and all of creation dwell and delight together, feasting forever in the presence of God.

As I talked about the gospel as a story of meals to my class, I ended by emphasizing God's use of eating as the main player in this entire narrative of history. While I've lost some of the naivety I held that day at age twenty-two (it turns out the food system is incredibly complex), I remain convinced that food is central to God's work in the world.

Theologian Norman Wirzba says it best in his book *Food and Faith: A Theology of Eating*: "We don't really understand food until we perceive, receive, and taste it in terms of its origin and end in God as the one who provides for, communes with, and ultimately reconciles creation." All of creation is a physical manifestation of God's love "made tastable and given for the good of another," as Wirzba says.[1] All of creation exists solely because the Lord desires a world full of delight.

The Creator carefully designed humans and animals with two primary needs: to draw nutrition and energy from food in order to sustain life and to find companionship in sharing life with others. The only thing God called "not good" in the initial act of creation was a human being alone. And because God created the world out of an overflow of delight, these most basic needs are fulfilled in the joyous act of commensality—eating together. Food is not just a collection of nutrients. Every bite of food is a full sensory experience, a combination of sight, smell, texture, and taste that draws people together. When we eat, we experience the delight of the created order, we experience the sensory magnificence of our human bodies, we commune with one another, and, through this connection with all of creation, we commune with and delight in our Creator as well.

The first humans failed to honor the limits that God set in place. "The fruits of that one tree," writes Alexander Schmemann, "was food whose eating was condemned to be communion with itself alone, and not with God. It is the image of the world loved for itself, and eating it is the image of life understood as an end in itself." Thus the "original sin" that took place that day was a ceasing to hunger after God and God alone. Ceasing to see every aspect of life as utterly dependent on an interdependent world as "a sacrament of communion with God."[2]

Relationships central to the created order were brought together through food. So it is no surprise then that our relationship to food continues to affect other areas of human brokenness. What God intended for flourishing brings unspeakable pain, as relationships are broken by the selfishness of that fateful bite. And yet, despite all their complicating factors, God chose to keep meals central in the restoration of the world.

When Jesus told his followers to remember him in the eating of bread, it was not because he happened to have bread and wine on hand. It was because the very act of eating together is central to God's purpose for creation, and in his death and resurrection Jesus invites us to take part in reclaiming food for good.

As I began my career in baking and pastry, whipping together cookie dough, piping buttercream, and balancing bakery budgets, I learned about the nuances and complexities of eating. I dropped my plans for a culinary arts degree, opting instead to study the history, culture, and public policy of food, expanding my vision of its role in the world. "Food is not an end in itself, but a means to many ends," says anthropologist E. N. Anderson.[3] "With so many needs to satisfy, and so many foods that can be used," he says, we simply cannot develop one simple recipe for good eating. The cycles of brokenness so infiltrate economic and cultural systems that no simple prescription exists that can shift creation back into place. On more than one occasion, I thought about letting go of all my cares about food and finding a new career path. But even as I discovered the growing complexity of the story, I remained drawn to the eucharistic table.

Many writers and theologians offer suggestions as to what it means to eat eucharistically. Theologian Jennifer Ayres says that "patterns of growing, sharing, and eating food are a means of revelation: they reveal something about the brokenness of humanity and its social and ecological arrangements."[4] At the eucharistic table, she says, we must ask what it means to work for justice while hoping for a new creation. "Inasmuch as our food system works against God's created order, poisoning bodies and landscapes, that system is demonic," maintains farmer and theologian Fred Bahnson. "It is a cruel parody of the way Jesus calls us to eat and live, and I believe it's one of the great forces at work against the Kingdom of God."[5]

At their core, these views recognize the interconnectedness of food, humanity, and all of creation. Fundamentally, these writers and thinkers long to see the deep brokenness of the world healed through our choices in food. They agree that food will be central to God's complete restoration of creation. A robust theology of eating entails challenging the injustice in the growth, production, and distribution of food. But given the complexities of farming, cooking, and eating, it can be overwhelming to know where to start.

Questions of time and affordability, personal taste, allergies and aversions, tradition and ethnicity, and availability and seasonality affect individuals' choices in food. These complexities make a simple prescription for eucharistic eating impossible. Instead, the questions beg Christians to push further into explorations of the ways that God communicates through food, beginning with the way God communicates throughout Scripture: in the practice of eating together.

Food, Anderson says, is "second only to language as a social communication system."[6] Around the world people mark their family history and ethnicity through cuisine, grounding their identity in the ways particular foods are prepared and consumed. Food tells stories of movement, of relationships, of place. Soul food, for instance, is a method of remembering a history of African American resilience. "The essence of black culture has been handed down through . . . the selection and preparation of soul food," writes Marvalene Hughes. "Expressions of love, nurturance, creativity. . . . Economic frustration and survival."[7]

Recipes tell embodied stories, allowing future generations to physically take part in the continuation of a memory. Recipes are "generational storytelling with an open mouth and heaping spoon," as Carolina Hinojosa-Cisneros calls them. "In meals, we find theology and sacredness; we find the hand of God moving. . . . All our worlds collide in one small kitchen overflowing with stories, backgrounds, culture, chisme, and never a bowl empty of salsa."[8]

It is this identity-forming, story-telling power of food that the Israelites harnessed in their annual practice of Passover, remembering God's faithfulness in deliverance from Egypt through the rituals and recipes of the meal. For Jews today, the Seder meal deepens the layers of the story. "The celebration of freedom brings to mind not only the Exodus," writes folklorist Sharon R. Sherman, "but the pogroms of Russia and Poland, the Holocaust, the Warsaw Ghetto uprising, the establishment of the State of Israel, the plight of the Ethiopian Black Jews. . . . All of these events become part of the tale and add new dimension . . . in memories evoked by the Seder."[9] Even as each individual item on the plate has acknowledged and deeply ingrained meanings, Sherman says, the ritual itself takes on further meaning each time a family participates in its rhythms.[10]

Jesus took this same Passover meal and reoriented its telling. By embedding new meaning into the established tradition, he sought to bind his followers together by tying the story of who they are into the process of sharing a particular kind of meal. He then commands his disciples to carry on his memory through a continued ministry of meals, staking their identity as Christ-followers in the sharing of food. He commemorates his body and blood in the bread and wine, using these specific elements to tell the story of his death and resurrection.

In the two thousand years since Jesus first established this meal, confusion over its purpose has been at the heart of fractures in the Christian church. Some Christians view the ritual as a place to establish boundaries of Christian versus non-Christian. Others view it as an embodied method of evangelism—bringing outsiders into community through the embodied process of eating.

This book doesn't attempt to resolve these questions and tensions or offer a "right" theology of the Eucharist, but instead it observes what happens when we eat together as an act of worship. What is clear, no matter your theological persuasion, is that Jesus wants folks to eat together in his name. Jesus wants his followers to eat bread, drink wine, and feed others and, in that way, to participate in the restoration of a deeply broken creation. For the church to authentically reclaim the practice of eating meals together, she must examine who feels welcome when the church gathers and what happens when people don't feel included. She must explore what people feel when they worship together over a meal and seek to understand the dynamics of comfort and power. Through this kind of meal-sharing Christians will commune with their Creator and invite others to commune as well.

2

On Beginnings

The Early Church

When we moved into our post-college home (fondly named Chez Heureuse—the happy house), my two roommates and I began hosting themed dinner parties. New to the area, we aimed to build a community in the city by connecting each others' friends from work, school, and church. We would choose a theme, brainstorm a set discussion question, and then invite two people we thought would be curious enough to participate. As expected, the evenings began awkwardly, with shuffled feet and unwanted silences. But over the course of the night, we engaged with questions both silly (Where would you travel in time?) and serious (What's one resolution you've kept?). We invited guests to share their stories with folks they'd only just met. As we did, new friendships formed, and in one case, we played matchmaker, as well.

After our inaugural dinner party, one guest, Daniel, reflected on how the experience powerfully bonded him to the others at the table: "I don't know where you're from, but I know your middle name and how you fell in love."

That fall, as I began graduate work in food studies at Boston University, in the midst of academic readings on food history, sustainability, and French gastronomic literature, Daniel's reflection lingered in my mind. How *does* the dinner table support the formation of friendship? I devoted the rest of my graduate work to the study of commensality, the social dynamics of eating together, in hopes of unlocking this mystery.

My studies began with understanding that eating together is an intimate act.

Eating is the most basic human function, critical to daily survival. But it's also one of life's greatest physical pleasures. To share this sensual process with others invites them to experience pleasure with us. It requires the sharing of our time and personal resources; it reveals taste preferences, table manners, and cooking skills (or a lack thereof); it creates the space to know others in a deep and different way than conversation alone allows.

Writers and chefs wax poetic about the beauty of the family dinner and the holiness of hospitality. I've read and written on the importance of inviting people to dine together. But *why* does it work? *How* do sitting around a table together and eating a plate of food create bonds between one another more powerfully than just sitting in a circle of chairs to chat? And can any random group of strangers sit down together and expect to emerge from the experience as friends?

Georg Simmel, a German sociologist of the early twentieth century, made observations about meals. Even though the meals he observed took place in a different cultural setting, his explanations of commensality remain relevant today. Eating together, he wrote, fosters community because everyone shares the need to eat. In general conversation, it might be difficult to find a common topic of interest to engage a diverse group of people. The weather is a common point of conversation in these awkward moments, compelling because it is felt by all. Similarly, eating is a basic function that everyone shares, so if nothing else, a group can sit around a table and talk about the very food they are consuming. Because food creates a basic level of connection for everyone, in theory, people who have nothing else in common can yet gather together over a meal.[1]

To test Simmel's theories, one spring I designed an experiment. I asked three women who did not know one another to commit to a series of meals in my home. They would keep a journal of the process, writing down what it felt like to form friendships over food. I asked them to let me know what moments felt uncomfortable and when things felt a bit more natural; we would discuss together what helped and what hindered their comfort around the meal in my home. I chose a group who had enough in common to likely get along, but with enough differences they'd never otherwise meet.

The first night was unbelievably awkward.

It turns out that setting a table for strangers with no sort of theme or agenda or structure is really weird. I set the table with my nicest dishes and wine stems and spent the full day cooking: a warm fennel and grapefruit salad, asparagus risotto, crusty sourdough from my favorite local bakery, a gooey brie, and a chocolate tahini cake. The dining room was small, but an ornate harp stood in the corner. One by one my friends arrived, still hesitant about this entire idea and unsure of what they'd gotten themselves into. As I finished up the cooking, everyone took seats around the table. Bottles of wine flowed steadily, but conversation started and stopped.

The last ladies-only dinner party I went to we ate risotto, one woman noted. Pause. And we talked for a time about our love of creamy rice.

I tapped my foot nervously, unsure how to put everyone at ease. When my plate was empty, I clung to my wine glass. Not so much to drink as to have something to hold.

That's a beautiful harp, someone commented.

I'm glad we're finally beginning to get some spring produce in. I've been waiting for asparagus, said another.

I journaled that evening how I wished I'd created discussion prompts or at least not made the house so formal. Over the coming weeks, I mixed things up. We cooked together, using recipes the other women had provided; we sat on the back porch and ate over candlelight. We dined at a restaurant down the street. At some points we laughed deep belly laughs on the porch and at others we fell silent, unsure of what to say. The women shared stories of how they'd met their partners, and we giggled over tales of our very worst dates. We talked about sustainable food systems and our deep love for Oreos. After a month, we all felt a bit more comfortable with one another, though it would be a stretch to call everyone good friends. But when they would run into one another on the street or the bus, they quickly told me about it. Together we reflected on the uniqueness of the experience and the ways it made us think.

Despite awkwardness and discomfort, the intimacy of eating together somehow bonded us. We became friends in an unexpected kind of way.

Jesus's ministry took place almost exclusively around the context of food. As he spoke, he served meals. He told parables about food. And then he asked his followers to eat together and to feed others. He asked them not to set tables just for those who looked like them and could reciprocate but for the "poor, the crippled, the lame, the blind" (Luke 14:12–14). Through stories of food, Jesus spoke in terms that everyone could understand, and by telling these stories around a dinner table, he addressed his followers' most basic needs.

Hospitality, the sharing of meals with strangers, was a divinely inspired and intentional activity for Christ and his followers. This partly came from the way the people of ancient Israel understood themselves as sojourners in a foreign land who, as the people of God, held a responsibility to care for all vulnerable strangers in their midst.[2] Jesus himself depended on the hospitality of others for most of his life. Like the Israelites, he viewed himself as simultaneously guest and host—throughout his sojourn on earth he extended hospitality to the most vulnerable men and women in his midst.

When the earliest Christians gathered together after Christ's death, doing so over a meal was a natural extension of Jesus's ministry. As Jesus did in his life on earth, they set tables that were intentionally nonhierarchical and that worked against social stratification. Stories of these early Christian gatherings are shared in the book of Acts as well as through the writings of historians, most notably the second-century writings of Tertullian. "They devoted themselves to the apostles' teaching and to the fellowship, to the breaking of bread and to prayer. . . . All the believers were together and had everything in common, they gave to anyone as he had need. . . . They broke bread together in their homes and ate together with glad and sincere hearts," according to the book of Acts (Acts 2:42–47).

Tertullian offers even more detail regarding the early church meals. The gatherings brought together aristocrats and slaves in genuine care for one another, he says. They opened and closed every meeting in prayer, feasting together and giving money to the community proportionate to their income. Through this economic sharing, they took care of the needs of the poor and the sick, they buried their dead and provided for the elderly. They spoke as though God was present with them, abiding at their table. They expressed a genuine love for one another that amazed those who observed it.[3]

At the time of Tertullian's writing, Roman fraternities were common places of gathering for aristocrats. Known for their debauchery, the clubs were the quintessential vision of wealth and excess. In contrast, the Christian gatherings brought the wealthy together with the poor to dine as equals. They lived out a mind-set of abundance, believing that when the rich and poor come together to share resources, there is enough for anyone who walks through the door.

Although the dinner table is often heralded for its ability to draw people together, idealizing it as a place where *everyone* feels welcome and all strangers become friends is unhealthy. The table can also be a powerful force to establish division. If not intentionally focused on equality, the table can create boundaries based on age, gender, or social standing. Divisions are not inherently bad—separating children and adults at Christmas dinner can provide much-needed respite for parents and fun conversation for kids. However, this tendency to divide means that table dynamics must be understood in order to intentionally develop community.

The early Christians who gathered together in the city of Corinth did not remain attuned to these divisive dynamics. Rather than sharing a meal together, breaking down the stratification of social status, the Corinthians ate their meals separately, without care for the full community. One member would go hungry while another got drunk, behaving far more like the Roman fraternities than followers of Christ. The apostle Paul chastised them for using the meal intended as a sign of God's abundance to instead separate the rich and poor. "When you eat this way," he tells them, "it is not Jesus's supper that you eat. You eat and drink judgment when you humiliate the poor in your community" (1 Cor. 11).

Simmel says the primary ingredient for a sociable meal is a communal commitment to get to know one another. Part of that commitment is an agreement to behave and converse according to the common denominator of gracious table behavior. Most of us don't draw up a contract and ask others to sign prior to each dinner party, committing to good topics of conversation and appropriate manners. But in those successful dinner parties, we do follow an unspoken code. We receive an invitation and automatically ask the host if we can bring dessert or a bottle of wine; we wait to take a bite until the hostess has been seated; we encourage the children to pass through the buffet line first. When the event is more formal than we are used to, we feel awkward if our behavior does not come naturally (have you ever stared at the three forks before you wondering which one to pick up first?). When someone at our table doesn't understand the code, we give them funny looks, and we label them messy or crude. This code is often taught to us over the course of many years, as we learn table manners or maybe attend cotillion, as we go to dinner party after dinner party and develop unconscious training in how to behave. We might not be able to list all of the rules or expectations, but we can feel when something is not right.

This "code," however, is not universal—ideas of what's polite and what's not can be specific to a family, culture, or region. For a dinner to successfully create community, thinking about these dynamics is necessary. When Jesus invited prostitutes and tax collectors to dinner and washed the feet of his disciples, he turned every social code of behavior on its head. He subverted all expectations of hierarchy so that his followers would commune together without dividing their group according to social class. Their only common denominator was the very basic need for food. And out of that need Jesus created an entirely new way of functioning together as community.

Today, worship services of every denomination follow different types of behavioral codes: When to sit, kneel, or stand. When to cross yourself or raise your hands. When to cry or sway or say "Hallelujah!" When to clap or how to pray. What to call Communion or the Eucharist or the Lord's Supper. For those who have grown up in a church, the code and language of that specific setting are learned unconsciously. But for those who have not developed such a training, stepping into a community can be awkward or even painful.

Holding a worship service over a simple meal subverts all expectations of behavior. It creates a setting where a community can come together out of the very basic need for food. It can challenge a church to use the Eucharist not only as a sign of God's abundance but also as a practice that uses God's abundance to bring together men and women from a variety of social backgrounds. Then, bonding over the sharing of a meal, the community can create new patterns of behavior, worshipping God through their care for one another, living out self-sacrificial communion as modeled in the life of Christ.

When Constantine merged church and state, he imperialized worship, turning the service into an elaborate and pompous affair.[4] Gatherings shifted from small circular spaces of equality to a hierarchical focus on church leaders. They became highly formal events reflecting political and economic power. The ornate churches reflected deep reverence for a powerful God, but the services took away the radical social subversion of meal-focused worship. The Reformation brought back much of the simplicity that Constantine took away, but it also emphasized a cerebral faith and linear thinking. Following Christ came to emphasize mentally accepting a series of doctrines over embodying the practice of eating together. Post-Reformation, holiness and hospitality didn't go hand in hand. The church valued asceticism, and thus for some, feasting together was understood as antithetical to pious worship. Worship over a meal was seen by many as too joyful, too focused on physical pleasure.[5]

Even as the church moved away from holding its primary service over the course of a meal, eating together has continued to remain an important aspect of community life for many Christians. John Wesley was inspired by the Agape Meals of Moravian Christians,[6] communal meals centered on prayer and the reading of Scripture. Some Wesleyan traditions continue to practice these meals, also called love feasts, which are understood as valuable service alternatives to a formal Communion when an ordained minister is not present to bless the elements. The fellowship meal of the black church has been central to community formation from the time of the slave era in the United States. "After the celebration of Holy Communion," says David Anderson Hooker, "enslaved Africans would socialize among themselves and have a large shared fellowship meal. Often husbands and wives, parents and children, kindred and homefolks were only able to re-connect with one another during these post-communion fellowship meals." As a result, "the fellowship meal became closely associated with the celebration of communion as a creative response to the hegemonic constraints of slave era religiosity."[7] The fellowship meal of black churches in America continues to serve as the center of community formation.

Crock-Pots and casserole dishes are staples of Baptist fellowship halls. Sunday potlucks, Wednesday night dinners, coffee hours, and holiday feasts are features of church communities of every background. "Protestants eat before church, after church, and occasionally during church," says religious historian Daniel Sack. "If you ask American Protestants why they go to church, they're likely to say that they go not for the doctrine or the ethics but for the community—a community usually built and sustained around food."[8]

But when these meals are separated from worship itself, when they are seen as wholly different from the sacrament of the Eucharist, the deep connection between meals and the gospel gets lost. Community is not just a nice addition to the life of faith; community is central to the very foundation of the faith. Christ established his church around the table, not in individual, disembodied souls. We proclaim to follow a triune God, the Creator, the Incarnate Word, and the Comforting Spirit who dwells with us still. But how can we worship our relational Lord if our worship itself doesn't build relationships?

When we understand a full meal together as communion, as worship, then we see that Christ is present in the most ordinary and mundane aspects of living, God is worshipped through the most basic of human functions, and the community and the food that sustain us grant us just a glimmer of the Kingdom of God on earth today.

Eating together is the most basic and intimate act. And eating together as worship is the way that Jesus commands us to know and remember and follow him.

"Do this whenever you are together," Jesus said in the final moments before his death. "*Do* this and remember me."

3

On Loneliness

Saint Lydia's

I often drive home from church in tears.

As a single woman living mostly among married couples and families, I often find Sundays the loneliest day of my week. When the words of the liturgy form on my lips, my voice joining with the hundred in my sanctuary, the thousands in my city, the millions that have prayed these prayers throughout history, I feel simultaneously vulnerable before God and deeply connected with those around me. I long to share myself—my fear, my excitement, my anxiety, my vulnerability before God—with those who offer me the bread and wine.

But when the service draws to a close, fellowship quickly dissolves as families break off for lunch. As I return to my car, the vulnerability of worship meets the isolation of singleness, and the depth of my loneliness rolls in salty drips down my cheeks.

I joke that in studying food I study sex as well. Eating is one of only two acts that employ all the senses at once; one of two acts necessary for the continuation of life; one of two acts that provide pleasure while addressing a need. When used well, eating has a powerful ability to bind a community together in joy, but when used irresponsibly it can tear a community apart in heartbreaking grief. Even as I joke, I'm convinced that these parallels reveal the important role food plays in our communities, evident as early as the Genesis narrative of creation. "Eating is more intimate than sex," says Norman Wirzba,[1] citing the deep communion that occurs when we take food into our body. Every time we eat, we take in another life to continue our own; the very molecules that make up food become a part of our bodies in order to nourish us. In this sense, eating is never a solo act.

This deep communion with God's creation simultaneously creates deep bonding with those who share the process of eating together, too. Sociologist Claude Fischler notes, "When absorbing a food, a subject absorbs at the same time salient features of the food. . . . If eating food makes one become more like that food, then those sharing the same food become more like each other."[2] In the same way, the intimacy of eating food that has been touched by another, whether in preparation or in service, develops bonds between eaters as well.

God ordered the world in such a way that our deep craving to be in communion with others and our physical need for nourishment are met in a manner that brings great delight, reflecting the joy God finds in our communion. When the early church met together over meals, they worshipped God through this deep knowledge of communal delight.

The loneliness afflicting our congregations is not unique to single folks. I've heard the laments of married friends enough to know there are different kinds of loneliness. And in experiencing the depth of intimacy that comes through communal eating, I am convinced that God's intention for addressing this communal desire for intimacy is for churches to gather around the table and eat.

It takes intentionality for a meal to address the emotional needs of its participants. Just as a disconnected sexual act can fulfill a physical desire without addressing the emotional needs behind it, a thoughtless meal can make a lonely guest's hunger even worse. Such vulnerability requires a balance of both tenderness and strength from its participants. We need the ability to accept the inevitable wounds of an imperfect community because the communion is worth the risk of pain. A church predicated on this vulnerability requires the pastoral care of someone who is humble, resilient, and wise. And those are the traits of Emily Scott, pastor of Saint Lydia's.

Loneliness is present in cities of all sizes, among men and women of all ages and marital statuses. In New York City, the dynamics of this isolation are unique. The logistics of traversing a vast city with complicated transit makes getting together with friends a feat of engineering. Constantly surrounded by people, one is tempted to seek shelter from the bustle of bodies by walling oneself off from community. Upon moving to Brooklyn, Emily quickly realized the difficulty of establishing a close community of friends in such a climate.

With her move to the city, Emily refused to part with her dining room table, a relatively large piece of furniture for her small studio apartment. Often considered unnecessary by city dwellers, dining tables were rare commodities among her friends. Still, Emily remained committed to hosting people in her home. She quickly noticed the intensity with which friends responded to the offer of a home-cooked meal, longing for a space to connect and belong. Emily realized the power of her dining table to build the intimate connections that New Yorkers crave.

Though she held a seminary degree and worked at a church as a worship director, Emily did not expect to explore the pastoral route herself. She'd long questioned what it would look like to offer church for those who were curious about the teachings but unsure how to engage. Watching friends react to the intimacy of the dinner table, Emily realized her call—to start a church built around the table.

During her time in seminary, Emily and her classmates held meals that they called "hearty Eucharist." Playing on the early church's practice of gathering together in one another's homes, they would set full tables with all kinds of food as a practice of Communion. As part of her theological training, Emily also spent time as an intern at Saint Gregory of Nyssa, where she took part in worshipful meals called Feasts of Friends. When she acknowledged the need in New York for worship over a meal, Emily found quick support among mentors and colleagues. She recognized the vulnerability necessary to start such a church, which inspired her to build a community of members so devoted to one another that they would continue to grow once she, as the pastor, stepped away. By modeling humility through her dependence on and trust in fellow church members, Emily formed a community committed to welcoming others into vulnerability as well. Woven into the very founding of Saint Lydia's is a realization that no aspect of church can be done alone.

Many food studies scholars express concern over the increasingly individualized approach to eating in modern

Western society. As food is driven further and further into the realm of commodity, it loses its social significance. Sociologist Claude Fischler laments that when we lose sight of the history or social significance of our food, we lose sight of our own identity. "If we do not know what we eat," he asks, "How can we know what we are?"[3]

Similarly, as Western Christianity moves into an increasingly individualized understanding of faith, we lose sight of ourselves as inherently communal. We lose sight of the long history of believers whose traditions we continue, and we forget the nuances of the story our meal of bread and wine must tell. If our churches do not know what happens when we eat together, how can we know what it means to be made one in the body and blood of Christ?

Embedded in Christ's command to eat together as the church is a provision for loneliness—not just the loneliness of social isolation, what sociologist Robert Weiss describes as the need for connection with other people, but the loneliness of emotional isolation—the need for deep intimacy and vulnerability.[4] One New Testament character who understood this call was a wealthy woman named Lydia, a "worshiper of God" and "a dealer of purple cloth." The Lord opened Lydia's heart to the words of the apostle Paul, the book of Acts says, and immediately she urged others to come into her home. To Lydia, following the ways of Christ meant promptly welcoming others in to feast, to sleep, and to find communion (Acts 16:11–15).

Like its namesake, Saint Lydia's church ushers in those who are hungry, tired, and lonely, welcoming them to find rest and belonging. Every week Emily stands outside the front door, clothed in collar and stole, to welcome folks in from the busy street. The church has held dinners in a variety of spaces over the course of its lifetime, but the biggest step towards permanence came when they moved into a space of their own in the Gowanus neighborhood of Brooklyn. The narrow storefront functions as a shared office space for freelancers throughout the week, building community around the table beyond the Sunday and Monday night services. A full wall of windows offers passersby a peek into the spiritual haven the church offers to isolated New Yorkers, with all tables pointing toward the small kitchen space in the back.

On Sunday and Monday evenings, the church works together to transform the meeting space into a sanctuary. The cook of the day puts the final touches on the meal while worshippers hustle to set the tables and prepare the space for worship. The scents of tomato soup and whole wheat bread permeate the room while the clanging of plates and silverware and the chatter of friends build anticipation for the dinner party about to begin. This preparation time is a vital aspect of worship—creating the space together gives everyone the opportunity to feel welcomed into the room. Everyone who joins the gathering comes with vastly different experiences of church, but common to them all is the desire for a space to question, challenge, and explore together what it means to live as Christ in the world.

When it is time for the service to begin, the group shifts into a large circle around the circumference of the room. Raising her arms, Emily sings the opening prayer: "Loving and gracious God, increase in us the gifts of faith, hope, and love; and, that we may obtain what you promise, make us love what you show us." The group processes together to the tables to light candles and break the loaves of steaming bread. "As grain was scattered across the hills, then gathered and made one in this bread, so may your church, scattered to the ends of the earth, be gathered and made one in your commonwealth."

The service is bookended by the elements of the Eucharist, opening with prayers to bless the bread and waiting until the end for grape juice. By sharing the ritual in such a manner, the entire meal in between each element becomes an act of Communion. *Holy food for Holy people*, Saint Lydia's liturgy says. There is no prompt, no topic of discussion that drives conversation around the table—just the encouragement to get to know one another. While it is common practice in New York to maintain an air of standoffishness, avoiding the intimacy everyone so desperately needs, at Saint Lydia's the walls come down, prompting earnest conversation.

Emily not only models this openness herself, but she also asks other leaders—from the deacons, to the song leaders and cooks—to share their fears, their excitement, and their needs as well. Because the sacred and the secular can never be separated from one another, the holy meal is an opportunity to dialogue about the mundanities of life. In turn, this acknowledges the sacredness of the deep need for community that exists among all who live in the city.

After a Scripture reading and brief sermon, Emily opens the floor for a time of response. Aiming to train worshippers in theological reflection, she creates the opportunity for doubts, questions, and concerns to be acknowledged and honored within the church. All develop their understanding of God through their personal experiences, and Emily hopes that the service teaches those who attend to honor that experience and to practice recognizing the ways it leads to spiritual formation.

Emily acknowledges that the service is intense. There is no sitting in the back unnoticed, no hurrying through worship without speaking a word to another. This is, of course, the point. And yet it is also its own sort of barrier to entry. It's a long service, asking congregants to give up an entire evening to worship. It's not a service for everyone, and it does not try to be. But for those who are searching for spirituality, for those who long for full-bodied communion, it is a place to rest in the knowledge that questions and concerns and deep longing for meaning are holy, are welcomed, and are good.

Saint Lydia's likes to define itself as a place that practices its faith before figuring out exactly what that means. This looks like showing up, eating, singing, and praying, trusting that God will work through the worship and will draw the community close. "God will change us and be revealed to us," their liturgy says, even as they admit they don't quite know or understand how that works.

It takes an insightful leader to facilitate a safe space for questions. Like sex, eating together in this context is a deeply vulnerable activity. And without knowing exactly what others will say, what wounds others bring into the room, the pastor must know how to respond, how to recognize the pain of others and shift conversation when it could lead to further ache. Bringing a natural and tender strength, Emily has the innate ability to thoughtfully lead. Yet in her humility, she does not take on the task alone. Throughout the life of the church, she has surrounded herself with mentors—pastors she could call when overwhelmed or exhausted and who could provide new ideas or talk her through concerns. Simultaneously, she has built the church to rely on deacons, music leaders, and cooks to help carry the burden. From the beginning, she envisioned the church's existence beyond herself. She tried to plan a community that would exist beyond her departure, whenever that time would come.

Nine years of leadership later, that time eventually came. Sensing her own need for rest and her beloved church's need to stand on its own, Emily said goodbye and left Saint Lydia's in order to discern her own next direction. But because Saint Lydia's was never intended for independence, only the interdependence that God calls good, the community relies on its communal strength, knowing it will never have to stand alone. "My hope is that there's kind of a DNA that's been set about the ritual," says Emily, "and they will take that and grow." Not only has this DNA allowed Saint Lydia's to thrive in Emily's absence, but it has also replicated itself in communities across the country. Almost everyone who pastors a dinner church cites Emily as at least part of their inspiration. Emily, too, has been encouraged to see the ways the concept plays itself out in other contexts—each expression unique, beautiful, and aware that it belongs within a framework of interdependent strength.

Before the service at Saint Lydia's draws to a close, before rounding out the eucharistic rite with the passing of the grape juice cup, the church works together to clean. With different tasks allotted to each congregant, from washing dishes to drying them, wiping tables, sweeping floors, and putting tables away, cleaning up becomes a continued form of worship. The smallest tasks are treated as the holy, important work that they are within this continued opportunity for conversation, this further mixing of the sacred and mundane. When the space is ready for the guests who will come in to work the next day, the church gathers for a few more songs and a sip of the grape juice that rounds out their eucharistic meal. Emily slips back out the front door, again speaking with every worshipper as he or she leaves, ushering each one back out to the busy Brooklyn street.

Perhaps like me, some members of the church walk home with cheeks stained by salty tears. Perhaps the vulnerability of the evening and the beauty of the liturgy spark a deep emotional response. But following the meal, where the intensity of physical and emotional needs is acknowledged and addressed, every person leaves with the knowledge of one deep truth: though they may be lonely, they are never alone.

4

On Dirt

Garden Church

When I moved to Boston as an adult, I tried planting a variety of vegetables in pots on the front patio of my second-floor apartment. Only a few of them sprouted, and I harvested a pepper or two. Recently, I attempted to grow a pot of radishes. I eat radishes almost every day—on salad, on toast, on ricotta cheese drizzled with olive oil. Whether they are pickled or raw, I love their unexpected spice. I eagerly purchased a packet of heirloom breakfast radish seeds, a beautiful pot for my patio, a bag of high-quality soil, and organic fertilizer—the kind that smells like fish and seaweed. After planting, I was surprised to see them sprout so soon. I marked the days off my calendar, reading that radishes take only twenty-four days to grow. When it came time to gather my bounty, I carefully pulled on the tender greens, only to discover rotted roots and zero vegetables.

As someone who centers her entire life on food, I am embarrassed that I'm incapable of growing my own.

On Dirt

Tending new life out of the ground is no simple task. It takes knowledge of the seasons, of the soil, of differing plant varieties. It takes practice, and patience, and a commitment to place. Having moved city to city and house to house, I've never remained anywhere long enough to know its particular growing needs or to learn the art of nurturing its soil. I assume that so long as I remember to water and place my pots in the sun, all will be well. In my impatience and fierce independence, I've failed to listen and learn from the wisdom of the gardeners in my life.

I like to think that instead I pour all of my nurturing energy into the kitchen. I let others grow so that I can cook. I can tend to my friends and family by providing a warm meal. But deep down, I'm ashamed of my inability to fulfill God's early command to humanity—to keep and till the earth. When I read through Revelation and meditate on the imagery of the tree of life, a tree whose leaves heal nations and that bears its fruit all year round, I wonder how much I'm missing by not personally going back to the source of my food. I wonder how much more eagerly I could look ahead to the promise of the new creation if I would dig my hands through the dirt as it is today. If I would take the time to meet God back in the garden, I wonder if I might better remember the delight for which humanity was created and better see the world around me as so very, very good.

Every worship service at the Garden Church begins with a reflection on the tree of life. As the Reverend Anna Woofenden places an icon of the tree on a tree-stump altar in the middle of her garden sanctuary, she reminds all who are gathered that this image is the impetus behind the work they do. They worship in a garden to commemorate the place where God first dwelt with humanity, among the fruit trees. And they look forward to the day when that is where God will dwell once again, when the leaves of the tree of life restore the relationships broken by the humans' catastrophic bite.

While in seminary, Anna envisioned herself planting a church focused on economic justice. She'd spent over a decade working with church starts and consulting others in new church-start movements. She'd been a part of churches that aimed to house thousands, following a step-by-step plan for building big congregations. But she knew that this model wouldn't sustain the American church into the future. Passionate about bringing together people from various socioeconomic backgrounds for worship, Anna hoped that food could be the key for leading a church into a sustainable future.

Eating together is an effective way to build relationships, but enjoying food around a table is not the only step to creating community out of a diverse group.

Getting down into the dirt to work together on hands and knees can powerfully level out differences as well. In many urban areas of America, immigrant families and elders hold the most knowledge of gardening and farming. However, rather than appreciate this wisdom, we privilege the wealthy, the young, and the educated. Increasingly, these favored young adults have a desire to garden but little awareness of how to work the ground. When brought together with youth to work side by side in the soil, those who are often pushed to the margins of society become teachers, reversing the expected dynamics of power and creating the space for new relationships to form.

Identifying the capacity of the garden to create connections between people from different socioeconomic backgrounds, Anna decided that she didn't need to just plant a church, she needed to get her hands into the dirt and plant vegetables as well. She hoped that by empowering those on the margins she could flip expectations of church leadership. That perhaps, even now, the leaves of vegetable plants could heal a town. Over the course of several years, Anna's vision for a garden-based church developed. After conducting a nationwide search for the best place to implement such an idea, her denomination—the Swedenborgian Church of North America—helped her settle on San Pedro, California.

San Pedro is a small neighborhood at the southern tip of Los Angeles. For the first half of the twentieth century, San Pedro's harbor housed the United States Navy's largest battleships. The main streets of the area's Old District lead from the port up a steep hill to a neighborhood of expensive homes. A few restaurants, a coffee shop, an art gallery, and a small theater line the streets of the main square, but in between these businesses empty storefronts tell the story of a once-thriving town struggling to return to its former glory.

Today, San Pedro is made up of many Hispanic and African American families who reside close to the port, while wealthier white families stay near the top of the hill. It is also home to a large population of men and women without stable housing. The desire to revitalize the streets of the Old District recently began drawing wealthy homeowners down the hill to frequent the town's restaurants, but it also has created friction within the community as homeowners blame their homeless neighbors for slow business.

In the middle of West Sixth Street, between rows of attached buildings, a small plot of land sat empty for over six years, gated off from passersby. Across from the plot, a coffee shop called Sacred Grounds welcomed folks experiencing homelessness, offering them a space to gather and rest. This land provided opportunity to address the neighborhood's deepest needs without pushing homeowners away. Anna hoped that the growth of new produce might bridge the divide between homeowners and homeless, turning those who once petitioned against their neighbors into their advocates. With this vision, in May of 2015, the Garden Church opened up the gates of the empty plot and invited neighbors in.

A rainbow of ribbons flutters in the front corner of the garden, each ribbon representing a unique prayer. Surrounded by a bed of pink and orange flowers, the serene corner beckons visitors to hang their petitions before God. It's the only bed in the church that grows plants for beauty rather than consumption. Across from the prayer garden, a giant statue of a Tyrannosaurus rex waves at folks wandering down the street. He is regularly adorned in some sort of costume to fit the season, from a simple flower crown to elaborate angel wings. Dino, as neighbors call him, faithfully stood guard over the plot through all of its empty years, and the children of San Pedro love the opportunity to finally come touch the friendly beast.

Throughout the week, the plot functions much like a community garden. The church holds open garden times when neighbors can drop by and volunteer to weed or water. During "Little Sprouts" hours, parents encourage their kids to play in the dirt. Picnic tables entice families to stop by and eat a snack during farmers' markets, and local musicians play in the garden during the neighborhood's monthly art show. In addition to these neighborhood events, several volunteers commit time each week to finishing up the tasks that require more skill, time, or direction than communal work hours can allow.

But on Sunday evenings, the space becomes a sanctuary. Anna stores all of the pieces of the altar in a basket during the week. She doesn't like to leave the altar decorated and open to the elements, and the basket allows the church to remain portable in case of bad weather. Just as the Israelites wandering in the desert remembered God's presence and faithfulness by setting up a tabernacle for worship wherever they stopped to camp, Anna opens each service by unpacking the basket, piece by piece: a candle, the reminder of the light of Christ, a light that shines in the darkness and is not overcome; a vial of water, because Jesus is the water of life that renews; and the bread and the cup, foreshadowing the feast that will soon be shared. Finally and importantly, she brings out the icon of the tree of life.

"When we gather here at the Garden Church," Anna says, "we remember that we gather because we believe that all should be fed in body, and mind, and spirit, and we want to cultivate a place that has those healing leaves. A place where more peace, and justice, and reconciliation, compassion, and hope can be cultivated together. When we gather around God's table," she says, "all are welcome to feed and to be fed."

Every Sunday gathering is split into three parts: Work Together, Worship Together, Eat Together. By opening each service with weeding, watering, and harvesting produce, the community reaffirms its desire to dismantle socioeconomic hierarchy. After sifting through the soil and completing the chores of the day, everyone gathers in the center of the garden for the liturgy. The dirt stuck under fingernails and mud caked onto boots remind them where they worship—though they are sitting in a circle of benches singing, reading Scripture, listening to a sermon quite like any other church service, these rhythms are no more holy than the worship of planting seeds together ten minutes before. Every aspect of the liturgy reflects on the interdependence of creation and the need for worship to reconcile the divisions that hinder it from flourishing. From prayers petitioning God to speak through the sounds of nature, to songs that declare God's goodness as revealed in diverse community, to language that centers worship on God's abundance as evidenced through the potluck meal to come, the service reminds all who gather that God's desire is for the restoration of community and for the tree of life to flourish and heal nations with its leaves.

In his book *Soil and Sacrament*, farmer and theologian Fred Bahnson writes of the need to grow good soil. Land is not just a natural resource, he says, it is "a living entity worthy of our deference and servitude, our watchfulness, and our best attempts at preservation." Many farmers and gardeners act as though they must find good soil before they can plant, he says, treating the soil as nothing more than a vessel in which their chemically fed crops can grow. But the wisest farmers flip this perspective and seek to grow healthy soil, trusting that well-tended ground will birth an abundant harvest and that the gardener can stand back to watch God's mystery unfold.[1] When the beautifully ordered interdependence of God's creation is preserved, new life is bound to thrive.

Humble, scrappy, and wise, Anna deliberately tends to her diverse soil. A pastor empowering her community to rely on one another's strengths, she steps back knowing that the needed work will get done. Rather than coordinate volunteers to read Scripture or serve grape juice during Communion, she opts for spontaneity, trusting that those who gather will step in as needed during the service. Some weeks, her parishioners will come sober and ready to work; at other times they come admitting their lack of control over alcohol or drugs. Some come for the stability that Garden Church offers, perhaps the only stable aspect of their lives.

Many who choose to participate in these vital roles each week are typically not people who would sign up ahead of time or get placed on a volunteer rotation. The tasks remain open to newcomers or folks with less predictable schedules and are fulfilled by those who find the responsibility deeply meaningful in that particular moment. This rhythm allows everyone the chance to take ownership of the community and use their unique gifts to serve.

Such gifts include the bubbly personality Derrick[2] uses to fill the task of "main inviter," welcoming everyone he meets to join the community, easily drawing new neighbors into the church. Or Travis's love for building compost. Sitting in the back of the garden while those around him sing, he methodically tears every plate and napkin into small pieces so that it can break down in the compost pile and feed the garden's soil.

A young high-schooler named James comes just to work the ground, or so he tells people. Even though he is the youngest regular churchgoer by over a decade, this community is the one place where James feels he belongs. He says that he can't find any good reason to believe in God, but as he patiently tends new life in the ground, others report they've watched God slowly tend life in him, too. Viola faithfully attends each leadership meeting and often volunteers to serve grape juice during Communion. With tender brown eyes and a soft smile, she offers each guest her blessing: "The cup of forgiveness shed for you." The ability to serve as a leader is just the empowerment she needs.

When the diverse interdependence of community is preserved, every member thrives.

The liturgical portion of the service ends with sharing the bread and juice of the Communion feast, but a song of abundance draws this fellowship out to the dinner tables as well: *There is enough, there is enough, there is enough and some to share.* The harmony spills onto the streets as more guests wander in to fill plates high with food. Each week, a different church member with access to a kitchen prepares an entree for the community. Several others contribute extra side dishes, as well, ensuring that there is indeed enough and some to share. For community members without homes, this weekly meal is typically the only opportunity to consume fresh produce. Salads, soup, and roasted vegetables overflow the abundant table. The church dreams of one day having access to a kitchen of their own so that everyone has the opportunity to cook. But for the moment, the Garden Church owns just a Crock-Pot—where one homeless member excitedly transforms the garden's bounty of tomatoes into her grandmother's favorite sauce.

Over the course of the two-and-one-half-hour service, dozens of men and women flow in and out of the garden. Some come just to work and others only to eat. In many churches, this kind of transience might be distracting, but for a community of folks who typically aren't comfortable with one another or in a religious setting, it is necessary to create space for people to ease in. With the church's gates open to the streets, worshippers can seamlessly come and go, stepping into the sanctuary as they are ready. The process of comfortably joining the community is different for members from various social backgrounds. Often, Anna has found, those without homes start by coming for dinner. After a few weeks, they might come for the tail end of worship in order to receive Communion, then eventually they arrive for all of worship, and finally they come to work as well. But for wealthier neighbors excited about the community garden aspect of the church, the flow works in the opposite direction. They first come to work, then eventually they stay on for worship and the meal. Like building healthy compost, the long process of breaking down a community's economic division is nearly impossible to observe. But the green sprouts emerging from the garden's soil are evidence that here in San Pedro new life is slowly taking hold.

While the crops are still small, their leaves have already begun to bring about healing. Faithfully blooming year-round in the California weather, they demonstrate God's presence and faithfulness in the garden. With each turning of the soil, relationships form among those who never would have thought to become friends. Week by week, they unpack their tabernacle and pray that, as they gather in the garden, they might foster fertile soil where the tree of life can take hold.

When we meet God here in the Garden Church, where carefully crafted ecosystems sing of the magnificence of creation, we catch a small glimpse of the beautiful dance of life and death that is slowly being restored. And it is so very, very good.

5

On Neighbors

Southside Abbey

No matter the time of day, the parking lot of my favorite grocery store is a maze of idling taxi cabs, large families pushing carts full of food, and cars attempting to find a parking spot. Inside, the checkout lines stretch all the way down each aisle—with an express lane weaving around the eggs, butter, and cheese. On any given shopping excursion, I spend about 15 percent of my time putting items in my basket and 85 percent waiting to walk over to the next aisle. It's a big boxy building full of fluorescent lights and advertisements that appear to have been printed in the early 1990s. This store maintains a reputation for great employee benefits and offers remarkably low prices. But these perks are not the primary reasons I choose to shop there. I go to Market Basket because it's where I see my neighbors.

Strolling through a farmers' market is a lovely way to spend a lazy Saturday morning. I know the best butchers, cheesemongers, and farmers in my area, and

I always enjoy talking with the men and women who grow my food—my friends who run the spice stall, the ice cream spot, the meade-maker, and the florist shop. But living in this city, I've watched my neighborhood transform with the introduction of specialty food stores and farmers' markets that stock local wares with trendy packaging. The folks who tend to shop at these spots look an awful lot like me: mostly white, mostly middle- to upper-class, mostly young with a college degree. To shop only in these outlets significantly alters the type of people with whom I come into contact. It is possible to live on my street, to shop at the specialty stores, and never come into contact with anyone who looks different than I do.

But when I go to Market Basket, I gain a robust picture of the faces that make up my neighborhood. Under the fluorescent lights of the supermarket I see the diverse range of men and women who also live on my street: immigrant women from India, Nepal, Brazil, and Haiti; young fathers with small children in tow; elderly couples who've lived in town since well before it was the "cool" place to be.

Where we choose to shop, the foods we choose to eat, and the people we invite to our tables significantly alter our understanding of who lives among us. Wandering the aisles of Market Basket, where each row is dedicated to neighbors from a different region of the world, I see the items that make my neighbors feel like they belong: the plantains, yucca, and passion fruit, the rose water and pomegranate molasses, the rice flour and teff, the hundreds of spices and blends. These items are also available for purchase at any number of specialty stores, made hip through special packaging and displays hoping to attract a cool crowd. But when each ingredient stands unassuming on the supermarket shelf, it's simply a balm to my many neighbors who long for a taste of home. Because my neighbors know that their choice foods are always within reach, this store tells them that they belong.

Precisely at 6:11 p.m. on most Friday evenings, a delivery person walks through the doors of Chattanooga's Hart Gallery carrying dozens of boxes of pizza. Pizza in an art gallery might sound like an odd juxtaposition, but the Tennessee gallery, like my favorite grocery store, doesn't use art to attract a high-class crowd.

The works of art hanging from the walls reflect the great skill of their makers, but the space doesn't come with unspoken expectations of behavior or artist statements that are obscure and from famed arts schools. The stories of men and women who make a living through their art are proudly on display; they are homeless and nontraditional artists who paint, sketch, sculpt, and make jewelry to express the places they call home. Throughout the week, the gallery offers classes and studio time for artists and is open for shoppers to stroll. But when it closes at 6:00 p.m. on Friday evenings, the gallery transforms into a sanctuary where the artists worship together with a host of other neighbors.

As the scent of cheese and pepperoni fills the gallery, children's eyes grow large with excitement. Pizza night at Southside Abbey is a favorite in this crowd. Tonight, as they do every Friday night, the church will feast. No belly will go home hungry after this meal.

Gathered around tables set up in the shape of a cross, the congregation breaks sub sandwiches, empanadas, or everyone's favorite, pizza, while worshipping through the liturgy of an Episcopal service.

The inspiration for Southside Abbey began with a funeral. Founding priest Bob Leopold wanted to share the love of God with his friends and neighbors who felt out of place in a traditional church setting. When his close friend died, the very group he longed to reach attended the funeral. Bob led the service as a celebration of life from the Book of Common Prayer. Surprised by a service proclaiming hope and joy, these friends and neighbors came to Bob reflecting their interest in a church that focused on the goodness of God.

"We can't improve on the biblical story of Jesus," Bob said. "We can't improve on this meal that God gave us." He decided it was necessary to rethink the structure of church to grasp the fullness of God's goodness. Gripped by the meal Jesus gave, Bob felt that there was no better way to rethink such a structure than around the dinner table. "We've so stylized this meal that we hardly recognize it as a meal anymore. I don't think the last supper looked like that, or that the early church looked like that." In order to reclaim the tradition, Bob felt it was important to make it a slow meal.

In its first year, Southside Abbey grew rapidly. They attracted crowds of young families, the coveted demographic of most church-planters. But these were not the primary neighbors whom Southside Abbey longed to reach. In their second year they prayed that God would expand their community. And with that prayer, trust grew and spread among those experiencing homelessness in Chattanooga. Hungry for a meal of dignity, neighbors began to come to the feast. But the coveted demographic that Southside Abbey had originally attracted didn't care for this congregational expansion. Citing fear for their children's safety, many families opted to leave. Despite the concern that drove many away, Bob held his commitment to his neighbors.

"Jesus promises all kinds of things, chiefly to be among us," Bob says. "But not ever safety. We think of the martyrs. They knew that safety was not on the table (in the world's terms) but this sort of safety that Jesus offers is home and love." Through this commitment to those who are hungry to be treated with dignity, Southside Abbey maintained its numbers, even as the demographics shifted. Jesus remained faithful to his promise of presence, revealing himself through the love and compassion of the church's newest members.

By the church's third year, when it became clear that Southside was a home to all of its neighbors, they expanded again but this time with families, homeowners, and students who longed to participate precisely because the church included their outdoor neighbors. So on a typical Friday, folks with PhDs sit alongside folks who cannot read, millionaires alongside those with no possessions; folks from Kenya, Russia, Guatemala, Burundi, and Sudan mingle with locals; folks who trust in the power of God stand alongside those who question whether that God even exists.

Safety has never been an issue at Southside Abbey.

Promptly at 6:11 p.m. the Southside Abbey service begins, giving the gallery just enough time to close up before being transformed into a church. Hungry parishioners carry tables from a back closet and surround the room in chairs while the food is delivered from the restaurant of choice. The leader of the day passes out sheets of paper marked with the carefully written Southside Liturgy. When Southside Abbey first began, the leadership team thoughtfully crafted a liturgy based on the order of the Book of Common Prayer that suited their new setting while honoring their Episcopal tradition.

"Everliving God, you have created us in your image and love us as your children," they open every week, acknowledging the image of God in every neighbor, no matter how different each appears. "Fulfill the potential of all things, grant us peace, and bring your Kingdom on earth as it is in heaven."

Shortly after launching Southside Abbey, Bob travelled from parish to parish around Chattanooga to share word about his church, inviting Christians around the city to take part through prayer, giving, or attendance. On one of his visits to a local church, Mary Frances Beesorchard heard his message and eagerly joined the gathering. Though she lives over an hour away from Chattanooga, every Friday she makes the drive with her two daughters to join in worship with those she now considers neighbors. Mary Frances and a few other long-time church participants make up the parish council, a team of lay people who lead the church. From the start, Southside Abbey aspired to give leadership to lay folks as much as possible. Bob recognized the gifts and talents of his congregation along with their desire to serve, and he aimed to develop a model that would thrive off the gifts of all who worship. After four years serving as the church's priest, he recognized his need to leave in order to strengthen the church in this vision of strong lay leadership.

While the church is now easing back into the leadership of a new priest, for three years they carried on without an ordained minister at the helm. In that season, whenever possible, the priest of a local parish would join the service to celebrate Eucharist. But on the in-between weeks, when the consecrated elements of bread and juice were not available to the congregation, Christ would consistently present himself in the scent of pepperoni and cheese.

After prayers of confession for all that separates and divides, both from one another and from the heart of God, the congregation excitedly announces, "The Peace of Christ dwell in all our hearts forever!" Neighbors stand and greet one another, offering hugs and handshakes. The peace of Christ spreads through the room with contagious joy. Their eager interactions draw them through the buffet line, where everyone piles plates high with food.

"First we pass the peace, then we pass the pizza," congregants joke.

The church has explored different methods of serving the meal. Sometimes they ask congregants to dish up plates for the people sitting next to them, encouraging everyone to think about their neighbors before themselves. At other times they pass dishes around the table family-style, and occasionally they walk through the line and serve themselves. As the crowd makes its way back from the buffet to the tables, their overflowing dishes signal the abundance they feel at Southside Abbey. Over the course of the meal, everyone tells stories about the past week. "Where have you seen God in the highs and lows?" Mary Frances asks after reading Scripture and sharing a quick sermon. Along with stories of seeing God through the kindness of friends, the compassion of strangers, or the guidance of a doctor, some point out the artwork hanging in the gallery. Others contrast the food with the meals they receive at other churches.

As is tradition with the consecrated bread and wine, which must be eaten or returned to the ground after a church takes Communion, Southside Abbey holds firmly to their motto of No Leftovers. No food gets tossed in the trash; there are always hungry parishioners willing to bring the remnants home. At Southside, the motto doesn't end with the food. A commitment to no leftovers means that no person gets overlooked or left behind. Everyone has a name, everyone is known by God, and it's the mission of the church to learn those names and proclaim their belonging in the house of God. This mission of belonging is important not only to those who have no other physical home, but it also transforms the lives of those with their own beds to go home to after the service.

"When you get to know anyone as family, it breaks your heart to see their suffering," says Mary Frances. The church mourns together when any one member aches. And the church rejoices together when any one member experiences great joy. They have rejoiced together over baptisms, over healings, over births, over sobriety. The church is a place where those who are in the midst of trouble find hope by talking with people on the other side.

"This place brings hope to the destitute, weary, and lonely," says John, one member who is now on the other side. "It brings hope to people who have found themselves in helpless situations. We share our faith, we don't demand. Southside Abbey is life in itself." John has been a part of the church since its inception, offering hope to dozens of congregants wrestling the same demons that haunted John's past. As Mary Frances deepened her relationship with fellow parishioners, offering rides after the service, she found that they were the inhabitants of the tents she always passed, set up under a bridge. She found that they were the folks hanging out in the library or on the steps outside. She found that as she walked down the streets, she knew these outdoor neighbors everywhere she turned. "Sitting down at a table together," she says, "has opened my eyes to see my neighbors where I've never really *seen* them before."

At Southside Abbey, a meal is not just a service to the homeless. It is a place of dignity where there is no separation between those who serve and those who are being served. "There's plenty of places folks could get a meal if they didn't have any other meals," Bob says about his early intentions for serving the community. "But a lot of it wouldn't be my first choice." Extending hospitality to these neighbors and serving a meal of dignity mean paying attention to their tastes and offering a meal that satisfies those desires. Southside Abbey is a place where neighbors come together to learn from one another, to see one another, to acknowledge their shared home in the house of God. "We're tearing down the walls," says Mary Frances, "then repurposing those bricks to build the kingdom."

While many congregants attend other churches for celebration of a formal Eucharist or for various meals offered during the week, all consider Southside Abbey to hold a unique role in their lives. It is a space where folks who are tired can get an hour of uninterrupted slumber. It is a space where those who want to speak can speak without being told to shut up. It is a space where the hungry can eat and carry leftovers home without the expectation that they will participate in aspects of worship with which they disagree. "Hospitality has a social necessity and expectation," Mary Frances comments, explaining why this space is so meaningful to those in attendance. "If you have guests, you have an obligation for care and protection." By understanding hospitality as the framework for worship, Southside Abbey understands their obligation to offer care and protection as key tasks of being a church.

The leaders of Southside Abbey trust that God knows the names and sees the needs of all who walk through the door. They strive to address those needs in whatever ways they can, but ultimately they trust that if they learn every name and feed Christ's sheep, they are doing precisely what they've been called to do. "If all they've gotten is a meal, that's important," says Mary Frances. A full belly and the knowledge that their name is known are what each member needs—from those living in mansions to those who sleep in tents.

On Neighbors

Every meal at Southside Abbey tells an important story. Over melted cheese and spicy pepperoni—the luxury food of choice for folks who come through the Hart Gallery doors—every neighbor learns that this church exists to address the need to belong. In a city so diverse and beautiful, all are welcome home in the house of God, a house decorated in nontraditional art, with the scent of pizza wafting in the air.

6

On Rest

Root and Branch

Many of us are drawn to the rhythms of a liturgical service. I love multisensory worship: incense, candles, and robes. And my full body craves participation in the liturgy through kneeling, bowing, and signing the cross. But while these practices taught me a great deal about the rhythms of the church calendar and the meaningfulness of embodied faith, it was one liturgy alone that taught me to embody Sabbath rest: the liturgy of baking sourdough bread.

For years I spent my Sunday mornings in bustling bakery kitchens, planning out the entire day in one-minute intervals: shape rolls while flatbread rises, scale out cakes while brioche mixes, scoop cookies while butter creams. I'd clock out of work, coffee in hand, and rush to church with flour still caked on my forehead. I yawned through prayers and dozed off during sermons and then jostled myself awake to kneel or to stand, anxious I might forget the days I volunteered to play with children or serve the post-church meal.

Wendell Berry in his short story "The Solemn Boy" tells of the life of a well-paced farmer named Tol: "It is a fact . . . that Tol never hurried. . . . It would have seemed to him a kind of sacrilege to rush through his work without getting the good of it."[1] In those days, unlike Tol, I rushed through both work and church without getting the good of either, until my body, after urging me to let go of my weekly sacrilege, shut down.

Forced to rest and take time to heal, I left the restaurant industry abruptly. Without work in a professional kitchen, my hands craved the feel of dough. I found myself, each Sunday morning, mixing a loaf of sourdough in my home kitchen. Rather than follow a recipe or replicate a flavor I'd made before, I would feel my way through the process: dropping starter into a bowl of water to check if it floated—the sign it's awake and ready to leaven dough—and mixing in various kinds of flour—wheat, rye, semolina, or the spent grains from a local brewery.

With the dough subject to the whims of the yeast and the temperature of my apartment, the importance of slowness in crafting bread began to seep into my bones. The slow process reminded me that it's only when dough is at rest that yeasts get to work, pulling the best flavor out of wheat. With each turn of the dough, stretching and folding the sticky mess until it slowly built enough strength to hold its shape, I learned the deep satisfaction of getting the good out of every step in the process.

As time passed I would still go to church dusted in flour, but rather than yawning my way through the service, I discovered that each collect and creed gave words to the prayers I'd been proclaiming through my hands hours before.

"Sabbath," Norman Wirzba writes, "is not a reprieve from life but the putting to an end of the restlessness that prevents deep engagement with it."[2] At the culmination of creation, God took the time to simply enjoy it. God rested out of a desire to simply be in and with the beloved creation, to enjoy the fruits of labor. God placed us on the earth to care for it and to enjoy. Yet, as we labor with our hands and worship with our mouths, Western culture rarely really values the enjoyment part. We escape from the beautiful wild of the woods, or the ocean, or the garden, or the farm to sing words of praise inside the walls of a church. We separate the worship of our creative God from the creation for which we give thanks. In turn, the rhythms of Sunday worship trigger stress over details or become thoughtless routine.

But from the earliest stories of Genesis we witness God taking a Sabbath rest and asking us to do the same. Sabbath rest ensures that we allow ourselves the space to take delight in the fruits of our labor. We are told to rest not in order to escape from life, but to set aside those distractions that keep us from engaging with it.

Tim Kim and Neil Ellingson love the rhythms of liturgy, too, and they know very well the exhaustion of running through the motions of Sunday worship without gleaning the good each step of the way. For that reason they desired to build a community that followed sustainable rhythms and prevented clergy burnout, avoiding the weekly sacrilege of rushing through worship. While they find deep communion in holding a service around the table, they ache at the thought of giving up traditional Sunday practices altogether. Aspiring to see the two forms—worship in a sanctuary and around the table—as mutually informative, Tim and Neil started Root and Branch Church. They have learned and shifted their practices along the way—no two services look just alike. Still, each day they settle more deeply into a vision of what it means to worship through rest.

On a Saturday evening gathering of Root and Branch, sticky with the humidity of a Chicago summer, Megan stands in the kitchen cutting up a watermelon while her friend Allison picks mint leaves. Most of the crowd gathering in Megan's backyard have been here before for the biweekly small group service, but there are a few new faces in the crowd. Everyone receives a task—fill pitchers with water, run next door to borrow more chairs, find cups for the wine. The noises of the city—of sirens blaring, children laughing, dogs barking—seep into the service as the group settles into their seats for prayer.

Each table service takes place in a church member's home during one of three time slots: Saturday evening, Sunday morning, or Sunday evening. As a result, the practicalities of every meeting differ depending on the host of the day. Some evenings might begin like the one described above—by hauling chairs over from the neighbors' homes in order to provide seating for everyone. Others might begin with sitting in the living room sipping coffee. As everyone gathers, they review their week together—telling stories of work or of school, catching up about recent business trips, or introducing the group to any guests whom congregants invited.

When it is time for the service to "officially" begin, the pastor of the particular site gathers everyone together, passing out laminated liturgy cards. Five congregants volunteer for a *DIY Diaconate* role: one person to preside over the hand washing, one to speak the words of the invocation and benediction, one to lead the sharing of the bread and the cup, one to read Scripture, and one to read a written reflection.

"We gather together the way Jesus of Nazareth did with his disciples and friends," they open in prayer.

"Washing them as a sign of emboldened love, saying 'If I, your Lord and Teacher, have washed your feet, you also ought to wash one another's feet.'" Passing around a bowl of water and a towel, everyone washes and dries the hands of their neighbors in preparation for the meal.

When Root and Branch first began meeting, they all would gather together in the same building week by week, alternating worship styles throughout the month—the first and third Sundays were reserved for a traditional service and the second and fourth weekends were devoted to dinner church. As the services grew, Tim and Neil faced mounting concerns: What gets lost when dinner worship gets too big? they asked themselves. Is a giant meal economically wise—is it even feasible? Could the needs of the congregation to build communion around a meal be better met in another venue? Even dinner church has the potential to get complicated. The logistics of planning a large meal can take away from the rest that table worship can provide. The primary purpose, Tim and Neil consistently remind themselves, is to build a life-giving community. "Not just to 'get in touch with the times'. Not to be stylish and up-to-date," says Tim. "It's about throwing off the shackles of un-reflective obedience to tradition."

A few years into the church's life, they realized that one communal dinner service could not truly provide the rest for which the service was intended. So they threw off the shackles of their dinner-church model and again decided to try something new. The remedy became meeting in one another's homes, shifting the responsibilities from week to week and allowing everyone the opportunity to host. They divided the biweekly dinner services into three small groups for a service called the Welcome Table. Over the course of three months, about ten congregants meet together every other week in one another's homes for worship around a meal. In this time, the group grows in trust and intimacy, making their way to everyone's homes and sampling a taste of each other's cooking. On the in-between weeks, they meet all together for communal worship. After a three-month period, the pastoral team shuffles groups around and the process begins again.

The services follow a weekly liturgical pattern, but in the comfort of a home, each meal adjusts to the rhythms of the lives of those who gather. Children giggle in one room and a cat wanders in and out of the circle of chairs. Structure doesn't hinder the realities of life; this service is as much about the worship found in rest and enjoyment of company as it is about liturgy.

Just as the liturgy of sourdough bread deepened my experience of the high liturgical forms, so the Welcome Table guides the Root and Branch community into closer communion on their traditional weeks too. By rotating the small groups every three months, the congregation of forty slowly deepens relationships among all members. At the same time, the Welcome Table weeks provide rest for Tim and Neil, offering a biweekly break from the rush of preparing a full traditional service. For the pace of Root and Branch to work, however, commitment to the process from both congregation and pastoral staff is key. Neil and Tim do not wish to offer a hip new service for whomever is available on any given week. They desire to foster deep community among those who commit to serving and dining with one another over a series of meals. Everyone is able to rest, but only if everyone is willing to commit to the rhythm, to the communal process of slowing down and getting the good out of every service.

After washing one another's hands, the group shares the bread of Communion together before serving up plates. As they eat, they continue the conversations from before the service, taking the time to catch up and continue sharing the mundanities of life together. For some, the time might be awkward. But Tim and Neil insist that this isn't problematic. We all need to be more willing to accept periods of discomfort, they believe. It is, after all, the only way that we will ever move into deeper vulnerability.

When Root and Branch began, Tim was skeptical about the concept of the dinner service. While he was eager to create a community that broke down barriers that keep people from church, he was hesitant, being in a hip, young city like Chicago, to create a "cool" type of space that would serve as a barrier to those who didn't fit the white, foodie type. As a Korean American, Tim experienced close ties to food throughout his childhood in church. Every service included eating together, and Tim acknowledged the depth of community that was built around that process. And yet he also experienced very poignantly the ways that food quickly became a type of social marker. Growing up, Tim faced criticism from his peers for the foods he ate—like the spicy fermented kimchi that caused classmates to turn up their nose in scorn. These same foods later became a high-class trend among the peers that had made fun of them before. Tim feared that a food-centered service could easily lose sight of simply delighting in God's creation and instead become a platform through which worshippers would try to outdo one another—proving their "coolness" through the foods they shared.

While the urban location of the church causes the congregation to skew toward young adults, a commitment to self-reflection permeates the community. Tim's original concerns encourage the congregation to regularly question whether they are using food to bring people together or just to tap into the latest trend. They practice an ongoing process of self-evaluation to counteract any dynamics that threaten to divide. "Do we welcome those who feel unwelcome in most church settings?" they ask themselves. "Do we welcome *all* who feel unwelcome, or only those who feel unwelcome for the reasons we deem cool?" This dedication to evaluation is woven into the rhythms of each Welcome Table service, most evident in the communal reflection time that takes place after the meal. Once everyone's plates are cleared, the group transitions into a time of reading and reflection modeled after the practice of Lectio Divina.

A contemplative practice of engaging with Scripture through repetitive reading, Lectio Divina probes the Holy Scripture again and again, as the words come alive and speak into contemporary life. With each reading of the selected passage, the practice of Lectio Divina focuses on a different question. *What words, images, or phrases stand out?* the reader will ponder after reading through the passage once or twice. *What light does it shed on my life?* the reader will question after reading it again. *What might God be asking me to do?* the reader will implore after meditating on the text another time or two.

When practiced communally, Lectio Divina provides the space for God to speak through a variety of voices.

One person might be struck by a particular word, image, or phrase that in turn helps another to understand what light it sheds on her or his own life. At Root and Branch, the group dialogue is often lively, and participants are comfortable addressing the ways they might disagree with each other's engagement of the text. "We want to train our congregation in how to do theological reflection," says Tim. The communal practice of Lectio Divina is a powerful way to form this skill. The group is not merely left on their own in this reflective process, however. Before each discussion, they recommit to a series of Holy Ground Rules—to giving and receiving welcome for different opinions; to being fully present even in doubts, fears, and failings, as well as convictions and joys; to responding through honest, open questions; to trusting and learning from times of silence; and to building an atmosphere of deep confidentiality in which everyone feels safe.

Either Tim or Neil is present to guide and to keep the service on track—offering unique insight or prodding with deeper questions and encouraging further reflection. It is important to Root and Branch that the Welcome Table practice differentiates itself from a Bible study or small group. Just as the liturgy of a traditional service forms worshippers in the practice of prayer and helps a congregation commune with the broader body of Christians, so does the liturgy of the Welcome Table form worshippers in the practice of hospitality and theological reflection so that they might carry this worship into the rest of their lives.

After a time of prayer, including a sung version of the Lord's Prayer, the group closes their formal time together with the sharing of the cup and a closing benediction. *Take and drink in the promise of new life*, the volunteer for the sharing of the cup says while passing around the wine or juice. Hugs, handshakes, and joyful exclamations of "Peace be with you!" signal the closing of the official service, but the evening carries on long after the service ends. Some folks help to clean dishes while others put chairs away. And a handful sit around and continue chatting late into the evening, until the yawns take over any ability to carry on coherent conversation. There's clearly no rush to end the service: it's a kind of sacrilege to rush through the meal without getting the good of it. The pace of the Welcome Table allows everyone to drink deeply from the good that flows out of every service, forming the congregation into close community through the rhythms of both table and tradition. When gathered together, the community does not rush through the prayers and practices; they slow down and delight in the process, allowing the liturgies to form them in love for all that God has made.

The church does not need more cool spaces. It does not need bigger, fancier buildings or coffee shops and stadium seating. The church needs rest, the kind of rest that comes in setting aside the time to get the good of a community. Even for pastors, especially for pastors, the church needs the ability to be a space of restoration. "It's very honest to say 'we're human, we need a break, this is a job,'" says Neil. "It's ironic because [pastors] provide a Sabbath, but we need Sabbath from Sabbath." Pastors and congregants alike can find this rest when they slow down to get the good of both church and work, dining together over a series of meals, enjoying the service of one another's homes and cooking, disagreeing over the implications of a passage of Scripture, praying for one another, washing one another's hands, and passing bread and wine around a circle.

Sourdough bread takes on the most flavor not through extra ingredients or hip, new techniques. It comes into fullness slowly, as the leaven works its way through the dough. The Kingdom of God is like leaven, the Gospel of Matthew says. It builds strength and develops flavor when we slow down and let the yeast do its work. At the culmination of creation, God set aside time to rest and delight in the good world God made. When we gather together as a church, we are called to this rest, too. We are called to be with one another. And in turn, we will work our way through the discomfort of difference and live into the purpose for which we were originally created: to delight in the world God made.

7

On Membership

Potluck Church

Growing up in Dallas, Texas, I was highly involved in our small (by Texas standards) evangelical church. This meant regular attendance at potluck lunches where the large community room would be lined with tables full of Crock-Pots and casseroles. The children found seats on the ground so that we could gobble up our food quickly before running off to play, while parents would sit around the tables for adult conversation. Our Sunday afternoons were filled with the simple pleasure of running around the church, finding hidden boxes of Goldfish crackers while mom and dad enjoyed an afternoon with their friends.

In this church we took Communion only once a month. At the front of the sanctuary, the ministers would set the white table engraved with the words "This do in remembrance of me." In a ceremony that extended the service by an extra ten to fifteen minutes, ushers would pass plates of oyster crackers and thimblefuls of grape juice down each aisle. All around me, adults would bow their heads before eating their sacramental meal. The solemnity of the moment around these two consumables confused me.

Partaking in Communion, I was told, was reserved for those who understood "what it meant"—but I was always curious how such a small bite of food could command such reverence in worship. One day, anxious to take part in the ritual, I snuck the elements while my parents weren't looking. I nibbled on the cracker and downed the shot of grape juice, but all I felt was dread inflicted by my over-active conscience. Later that afternoon, I sulked to my parents' bedroom to offer a tearful confession. As we talked about the events that took place during Jesus's final meal, Mom and Dad offered the absolution that I craved. Months later, I could articulate Christ's actions enough that the church allowed me to take part as well, but month after month I never really understood why it was such a solemn affair.

Years later while in college, I attended a charismatic church that met in an elementary school gym. The worship often carried on for two hours or more, everyone packed into the makeshift sanctuary with eyes closed and arms raised. People gathered in groups of two or three to pray, opening up to strangers with intimate details of their life in trust that God's presence would bring healing. It was a young church, made up mostly of students and young families, a cool crowd of folks wearing skinny jeans and hip haircuts. Energy pulsed through the room of men and women eager to feel the Holy Spirit move.

One Sunday as I walked to the service with a few friends, one of the women in our group announced it would be her final Sunday attending the church with us. We'd been attending for six months and were yet to take Communion. As much as she loved the community and the service, she explained, she could not attend a church that did not serve the Lord's Supper. And again, although I could articulate the story that explained why we ate the bread and wine, I still could not grasp why it was so important that it would draw my friend away from this church that we loved.

A few weeks later, in the middle of our worship, the priest of a nearby Anglican church came bursting in through the back doors, still clothed in his long robe and stole from the high liturgical service he'd just completed. Tears streamed down his face. "I left a service down the road where all the leaders are in long robes like mine, and our worship doesn't look anything like yours," he blubbered. I'd always assumed the ceremonial clothing, the repetitive prayers, and the weekly Eucharist of their service represented the height of the Christian solemnity I could not comprehend. I'd assumed they relied on movements and scripts to avoid confrontation with feelings. Then I was gripped by the words he muttered in between tears: "When I walked through those doors I was hit with the power of the fact that the Holy Spirit I so tangibly experience in our worship down the road is the exact same Holy Spirit here with you all as well."

I continued attending the charismatic church for another year, still unsure why the lack of Communion mattered so much to my friend. I loved the freedom to worship with my entire body—swaying, crying, waving my arms unashamedly to the music. I loved the surety with which everyone around me believed God to be present in the room. But as someone who experiences emotions deeply, I began to realize I was confusing my own fears, joys, and anxieties with the presence of the Holy Spirit. I found myself week after week afraid to step into the elementary school gym, unsure of the thoughts or feelings that would sweep over me once inside. As my concerns increased, I longed for worship that grounded me no matter the emotions that I carried into the sanctuary. Though I couldn't articulate it yet, my belly groaned for the solidness of bread and wine.

Skeptical of the rote ritual of liturgical worship, but too anxious to return to the elementary school gym, I visited the church of that crying Anglican priest. I fumbled through the prayers, and I watched in surprise as those around me marked themselves with the sign of the cross. In the routine, I found soothing for my emotion-driven concerns. Then I opened my palms and devoured a piece of sweet, wheat bread. Behind the robes and within the hymns, I encountered the same Holy Spirit who was pulsing through my church down the road. But in the meal, I consumed the grounding I so desired. I returned, week after week, discovering that no matter the emotions I brought into the place, I left with my belly full of the promise of Christ's calming presence.

It's been twenty years since I stole my first bite of Communion, and I've only just begun to grasp what it means to worship at Christ's table. As I probed further and further into the full-bodied worship of the Angli-can tradition, I learned the importance of what took place back in my small Texas church: While we sat in those crimson pews, a cracker and juice served as sym-bols of Christ's death. The potluck afterwards, though, was where our church really embodied the sacrament's meaning.

Every Wednesday night, fifteen or so members of Pot-luck Church wander through the gym of a large Mad-isonville, Kentucky, church to find a seat in the small basement room that has become their sanctuary. By the time the congregation starts to arrive, Pastor Rachel Nance has been in the room for half an hour, transforming the space from classroom to dining room, gathering stacks of plates from the church kitchen, and transporting tables from the gym. She has unpacked the basket of tablecloths and napkins, a candle, rocks, a chalice and plate—the entirety of Potluck Church's possessions—and has set one place at the table. A spot for Jesus, where a plate of bread and chalice of grape juice remind all who gather of Christ's continual presence at the table.

Other members slowly trickle in to help, filling pitchers of water, finding stacks of silverware, and, most importantly, loading the buffet table with their weekly offerings. The line overflows with gifts of salads, casseroles, chips, soda, and cakes. When the crowd swells in size to more guests than the dozen spots at the table, everyone rearranges the room to make space for additional seats. The Jesus spot gets shuffled around until there is room for everyone to eat, yet still no one sits in the Holy seat.

Rachel began dreaming of a potluck church on a Maundy Thursday in seminary. Exhausted from Holy Week preparation, she and her housemates opted to skip their church's service. Instead, they cobbled together a feast in the comfort of their home.

"I've got some bread," one friend remarked.

"I've got cheese," added another.

"I can bring wine!" offered a third.

Everyone brought together the elements they had to offer and feasted late into the night, remembering Jesus's final meal with his disciples. They served one another bread and wine, celebrating the night that Jesus instituted the meal shared by Christians ever since. But what Rachel remembers most from that evening is the depth of conversation. It was around this dinner table, in their simple act of worship, that this house of seminarians explored together the theological questions gnawing at their hearts, finding their conversation focused equally on the spiritual and mundane.

"What if church was like this?" Rachel dreamed. For nearly a decade the question percolated in Rachel's mind. What made that night so special, she asked herself, and how could it be captured weekly, as church? She tested her idea of a potluck service on subsequent Maundy Thursdays, but she never let go of her dream of holding a dinner service every week. Finally, she and her husband decided there was nothing to lose; it was time to test this crazy idea.

As a pastor within the Disciples of Christ denomination, Rachel stands in a tradition that has long desired to return worship to the simplicity of the early church. Trained to look to the book of Acts for direction and inspiration, Rachel clung to the passages describing meal-centered worship among the first Christians. With a rising interest in similar methods of worship emerging across the country, she looked to contemporary communities who shared her vision of restoring this ancient practice.

But departing from the models she observed popping up across the country, Rachel believed the potluck itself to be a necessary component of worship. At Potluck Church, everybody brings something. Even if it is a persimmon found on the ground, a box received from the food bank, or a bag of fried chicken prepared at the grocery story, everybody brings something. By creating a setting to which everyone contributes, the potluck table manifests the equality of all who gather.

"You can see what's going on in the community or what's going in our lives by the food that we bring," Rachel says.

"We light this candle to remind us that Christ is present with us," Rachel begins as everyone hushes to silence around her. A congregant prays a blessing before ushering everyone through the buffet line. With plates piled high, the congregants chat about the dishes they brought and update one another on both exciting and mundane aspects of their lives. The group is small enough that everyone can fit around the same circle of tables, taking part in a single group conversation.

"Where did you see God at work since we last met?" Rachel asks, moving conversation in the direction of the service. Stories of interactions with strangers, of time spent in the garden, and of worship on Sunday morning reveal the desire to commune with God in all areas of life. "I feel like Potluck just weaves in and out of our lives all week," says a woman named Tina, recounting the ways God speaks to her day after day. Interspersed with each reflection on God's presence are compliments about the buffalo dip—both the spicy and the not-spicy versions that Alice brought to appease different palates—and jokes about the neon cake frosting that dyes everyone's teeth blue. Rachel leads the group in a communal reading of Scripture and a series of questions for reflection. "Feel free to interrupt me, as you often do," she tells the group before launching into a brief sermon.

Together the church asks difficult questions of the text at hand and allows the text to ask difficult questions of them as well. Conversation flows between serious and silly, giggles erupting every time someone makes a serious statement with a mouth of neon blue. This laughter doesn't detract from the depth of conversation; instead it reminds the group of the joy that undergirds even the most difficult topics of discussion. Just as everyone brought a dish to the potluck table, everyone brings insight into the conversation, as well. The group spends over an hour probing a small passage from the New Testament, getting up to refill plates and glasses again and again. Aware of the time, Rachel eventually draws the lively conversations to a close, though the discussion is always far from complete. Everyone agrees to pause the debate, knowing the chatter and laughter will continue after the service ends. Cleaning up, they cheer, is really the best part.

"What is your prayer?" Rachel asks, creating a transition for the group. Pleas for children, for safety in travels, for incarcerated friends, and for provision of food are brought to the table. Only as the varying needs of the community come to light in this time of prayer does the range of economic and educational backgrounds present begin to appear. "You wouldn't know by looking in the room," Rachel says later, describing the congregation, "but the former Madisonville mayor worships alongside folks who struggle to pay their monthly rent." In this space, the diverse needs are not only heard and lifted up to God together, but methods for responding to those needs are offered as well. And on those weeks when some members choose to keep concerns to themselves, their potluck offering can still provide unspoken insight into what's going on.

Originally, Rachel hoped to meet somewhere outside of a traditional church. She feared that the building itself would concern those with whom she most desired to connect—people who had been hurt by the church. Could Potluck Church rehabilitate the wounded if it required first that they step into the place of deep pain? But when her childhood congregation offered a free meeting space in the basement, with handicap accessibility, she took their support, and their wheelchair ramp, as affirmation that this was the space where they were called to worship. So far as they can see, the steeple looming above their heads has not hindered those seeking refuge at the table.

In preparation for Communion, one member reads a poem by Wendell Berry followed by the words of institution and a prayer to bless the bread. The lively crowd shifts into a solemn mode, breaking off a piece from the loaf as it's passed around the table and dipping their bite into the cup that also makes its round.

"Whoever shows up is Potluck Church," Rachel says every week to close. "And we are grateful you are here. God be with us until we meet again."

Eager to fill their table with people who are hurting and broken, Rachel realized early on a need for balance. A church full of the wounded could only offer healing if it also held the wisdom and encouragement of people who were at peace and mature in their faith journey, too. Grateful for the ongoing support of the senior minister of her home church, she asked not only for the space to meet but for a seed team of worshippers, as well. While many clergy might fear that such a request would shrink their own congregations, her minister's immediate response was, "Who do you want?"

Together they discerned a group of men and women equipped for such a role, approaching each individual with the request that they be a part of *both* congregations. Those who attend both the Sunday service at the host church and the Wednesday service at Potluck Church describe Sunday as the time they serve and Wednesday as the time they get fed, building a symbiotic relationship out of a position where turf wars could often reign.

As Potluck Church grows, they continue to ask God's guidance for the direction they must go. They cling to a vision of serving the deepest needs of their city, such as the opioid addictions that tear apart the lives of their neighbors and friends. They question how they can maintain the intimacy of their meetings without becoming so inwardly focused that it is difficult for new faces to break in. They question how to start new services while remaining entirely volunteer-led. Despite the unknown future, they remain at peace with their primary call of eating together at Christ's table. Week after week they see community deepen between men and women from many backgrounds, between folks who come because they so deeply love Jesus they want to spend all the time they can at his table and folks who come because they ache so deeply that they need a fistful of bread as a reminder that Jesus exists at all. They watch the remembering of a body made up of different skills, needs, desires, and prayers.

While the solemn passing of the bread and cup represents feasting on and with the present Christ, it is the potluck that embodies true Communion. Everyone brings something to the table, everyone is welcome and equal here. Christ dwells at the table where laughter and sadness intermingle, where there is inseparability of the spiritual and the mundane.

No one needs to articulate here "what it means" because their laughter says it all. "I'm just a person who happens to love Christ and anything to do with following Him!" says one member named Joy. Behind the tablecloths and within the giggles, the church encounters the same Holy Spirit who is pulsing in the sanctuary upstairs. In the potluck meal, the congregation assures one another that they are grounded in community held together by the spot set for Jesus.

Week after week they return to discover that, no matter the emotions they bring into the room, they leave belly-full of the promise of Christ's presence. Sometimes that promise tastes like buffalo dip and neon frosting that dyes teeth blue. Sometimes it feels like the curiosity that drives a young child to reach for a Communion cracker and juice. Always, it's a reminder that the same Holy Spirit guiding worship in the liturgical rhythms and the elementary school gyms abides at the table and in the bread and grape juice, too.

8

On Feasting

Community Dinners

At my church home in Boston, we spend every week-
end of Eastertide (the Christian season that stretches
from Easter Sunday to Pentecost) feasting together as a
community. Each week we gather in a different neighborhood, stuffing more than a hundred people into a
tiny city apartment to share a potluck feast. It is a time
for folks from different services or different neighborhoods or different life stages to mingle and to take care
of one another's kids. It is a time for folks who are food-
insecure to know they can find a hearty meal and those
who are lonely to know they will have a place for community. It is a time of healing for those who feel lost or
out of place on Sunday mornings, a time of bonding for
those who are new to the city, and a time of goodbyes
for those who will soon leave. Every year, the season of
feasting breathes new energy into the community, deepening relationships between pastors, small group leaders, church members, and new guests.

Feasting is a time to delight in the abundance of God's creation and to commune with God as well. It is a reminder that God not only provides for our basic needs but also chooses to address those needs through conviviality, pleasure, and bountiful celebration of food, family, and friends. It's a radical action, proclaiming that even in the midst of suffering God restores creation, and it's worth celebrating the pleasure of the world even now.

Feasting is intended to be not a celebration of gluttony or indulgence but a time to delight in God's creation of good food and loving community. Episcopal priest and avid home chef Robert Farrar Capon says, "Food is the daily sacrament of unnecessary goodness, ordained for a continual remembrance that the world will always be more delicious than it is useful."[1]

In Jesus's miraculous provision of food and drink— from turning water into wine at a wedding in Cana to the feeding of five thousand men and their families on the hillsides—Jesus affirms this sacramentality of unnecessary goodness. He doesn't just provide decent wine for the wedding guests, he provides an abundance of the very best quality. He doesn't just satiate the hunger of the crowds, he turns five loaves and two fish into a meal with baskets and baskets of leftovers.

When we look at the people with whom Jesus feasted the most, we see him consistently at the table with the poor, the lonely, and the most overlooked members of society. Jesus feasted with the most vulnerable not merely because he felt a conviction to feed the poor, but because he *delighted* in their very presence.

Founder of the world's largest gang-intervention and rehabilitation program, Father Gregory Boyle says, "Because those on the margins have been cut off, have been hurt, have been lonely, God views them as trustworthy guides into the kinship God desires. So we go to the margins because there we will find the people who can lead us into our own salvation."[2] Those society presses to the margins are the very center of God's world.

If Jesus found such deep delight in feasting with those cast aside by society, is it any surprise that the Holy Spirit continues to dwell and find joy among the same?

Seattle pastors Verlon and Melodee Fosner don't think so. Captivated by Jesus's meals with the poor, they realized that the church they pastored in Seattle actually bore little resemblance to the model set forth by Christ. Longing to follow Jesus's example, they set to work reforming their eighty-five-year-old congregation, turning a gathering of middle-class families into a feast for the homeless, the lonely, and the sick. As they turned their focus away from giving campaigns, membership goals, and measurements of spiritual growth and turned it toward cooking, eating, and loving those at the table instead, they found freedom and delight in watching the Holy Spirit transform lives.

What began as a vision for one church location has spread across all of Seattle. You can spot a Community Dinners service by its signature placard on the sidewalk—a sign with an image of a plate and silverware—as well as by the line gathering outside its doors. Each service draws around 150 people, 90 percent of whom do not have stable access to food or housing. These guests line the sidewalks along with all of their belongings, eager for the doors to open.

Community Dinners hosts a feast in neighborhoods all over Seattle. They currently offer services seven nights a week in seven different areas, with a goal of eventually moving into every neighborhood in the city. Rather than in church buildings, the gatherings take place in community centers, which are often less threatening to those who have felt hurt or rejected by churches in the past.

Once the doors open, volunteers usher the long line of hungry individuals through an abundant buffet: dozens of pans of lasagna, a giant bowl of salad, garlic bread, ice cream, cookies, and iced tea. A feast for everyone, a celebration of God's abundance all around. All are welcomed to walk through the line as many times as they please, feasting until they cannot eat anymore. A musician performs in the corner, providing background music to ease any tension in the room, while an artist paints a piece to reflect the experience of the community.

While plenty of churches eat together after their services, very few do so with the intention of drawing in those who are hungry. And plenty of soup kitchens offer meals to folks without homes, but rarely do men and women with secure incomes attend to eat and enjoy the communion. But Jesus did not separate the practice of feeding the hungry from that of feasting with friends. He enjoyed communion with them all. Dismantling the social stratification of meals was, in fact, one of his main intentions. Jesus hosted dinner parties that turned the forgotten into guests of honor.

Each Community Dinners service is prepared by a site pastor and his or her team of volunteers. The volunteer crew, made up of local students, members of other nearby churches, and regular Community Dinners attendees, prepares the meals at a prep kitchen in the Fosners' original church building. While the site pastor spends time talking and praying with the night's dinner guests, the volunteers set up the buffet line and serve all who come through. They pile plates high with the rich array: fresh bread smothered in butter, pasta spiced with oregano and basil, ice cream squished between chocolate chip cookies.

Each pastor, all of whom are bivocational, devote one day per week to his or her site. As they get to know the folks that regularly attend, they identify men and women who might enjoy participating on the volunteer team. Verlon and Melodee strive to see that Community Dinners functions as a church, not a soup kitchen. Building community among those from varying socioeconomic backgrounds is central to Christ's ministry, and therefore, they say, must be central to the ministry of any church.

In order to lessen the divide between leaders and attendees, every volunteer takes a break from serving to sit and join in mealtime conversation with those at the table. They too feast on a plate of gooey lasagna and crisp salad. The feast only functions to create true community when *everyone* eats together, host and guest alike. As they all settle into their seats, the pastor stands to offer a brief sermon focused on the gospel narrative of Christ's death, resurrection, and redemption. Some folks wander back through the line for seconds and thirds, their hunger drowning out the message offered on the other side of the room. While the proclamation of the gospel is important to the Community Dinners service, the spiritual practice of feasting tells far more about the abundance of

God's love than a sermon ever could. It doesn't concern the pastors if folks keep eating and ignore the sermon— they realize that the journey toward communion with Christ looks different for everyone.

The Community Dinners model is built out of the assumption that the Holy Spirit is in fact present during each and every meal, and through this communion the Spirit leads men and women into wholeness and freedom. By giving this responsibility back to God, the pastors say, they rest from the pressures of pastoral care. Their primary responsibility is not to convert but simply to listen, to feast, and to pray. Evangelism—sharing the story of the gospel—is important to Community Dinners. However, through the guests that attend their meals, the church has learned to rethink the way this practice has historically been done. They've witnessed the importance of affirming the dignity and inherent equality of all those gathered, no matter their difference in economic status, educational background, or religious understanding.

At Community Dinners, listening is always central. The pastors host in awareness that the Holy Spirit is already present among those who gather. While the language the guests employ might differ from what was common in the Fosners' original church, these conversations regularly reveal that the men and women who attend already know God, whether or not they have ever heard the story of Christ's death and resurrection before.

By feeding the hungry and housing the unhoused, the Fosners take Jesus's words in the Gospel of Matthew seriously: "Whatever you do for the least of these, you do for me" (Matt. 25:40). They center their ministry in the understanding that they are feeding and housing Christ himself. "Of course Jesus is out among the people who walk into the doors of Community Dinners," they say. "Where else would he be?" It is no surprise, then, that many of these dinner guests who have never even set foot in a traditional worship service can poignantly articulate their understanding of spiritual things. The church leaders, Verlon has discovered, are the ones who must learn how to listen. Such listening takes place naturally when gathered around the table, where conversations about the mundanities of life naturally arise like the scent of roasted garlic permeating the air.

Many Community Dinners attendees spend their days overlooked by everyone who passes by. But at the table they experience community, where their personhood, their stories, their reflection of the Image of God matters. Over time conversation naturally deepens—inevitably leading to a discussion about the limitations and hardships of life. In these conversations, the pastors recognize their own commonality with every church member. They bond over their shared experiences of pain and limitation. The pastors listen to the deep hurting of those around them. Rather than press an easy fix—Jesus is the answer to all our problems!—they respond by revealing their own fears and frustration. Most often they find the vulnerability of a shared meal fosters honest conversations between pastors and the church. And the joy and companionship of feasting express the abundant delight of God far more than uttering the script of any evangelistic tract.

"Growing up, we had pews full of broken people but it was taboo to talk about it," says Brian, one Community Dinners site leader whose tattoos tell the story of God's transformation in his own life. "If someone did talk about their brokenness, we'd brush them under the rug. So at Community Dinners, it's like we've lifted up the rug. How many churches will let a pastor preach about his brokenness and the room be okay with that?"

"For a long time, I felt the pressure that *I* had to bring something big to the table," says Will, another site leader. "My job has shifted to asking 'What is Jesus up to?' and to making sure I'm listening. Sometimes it's scarily easy!"

The team has identified dozens of neighborhoods around Seattle where more than a third of the population is in the lower-third income bracket of the city. These "sore neighborhoods," as Verlon has named them, often don't appear to be places of want, but the hungry live in the shadows of expensive homes and trendy restaurants. The goal of Community Dinners is to launch services in every neighborhood on this list—feasting with hungry residents all across town.

Verlon and Melodee have slowly passed the leadership of each site on to other pastors, focusing their own energy on training new leaders around the world. In his meals during his time on earth, "Jesus implanted both the message and the manner of working it out in culture," Verlon says, "and that should never be questioned. It is valuable for us to note what God has established that is timeless by design. The more we understand the deep roots of Jesus's dinner table, the more beautiful it becomes." To Verlon, holding church around the table is not an evangelistic tool, a package through which to share the message of the gospel. Eating with others embodies the gospel, the message of which is rendered meaningless when void of any physical expression of care.

"Jesus's strategy of rescuing the world didn't involve talking about spirituality. It involved having dinner with sinners, caring for people. The Church is not meant to be a purity system or information download. It is meant to be a rescue expression—Christ's rescuing all of creation back to the purpose for which it was created. We are guilty of being so heavenly minded that we're of no earthly good. We are primed by theology and ignorant of sociology. Jesus very much believed that he wasn't handing over just the message but also the way it would be done," he says.

Verlon envisions the dinner-church model transforming the work of the church around the world, providing for the needs of neighbors through feasting together. How can anyone sit and listen to a lesson about God's love and provision, Verlon questions, when all they can think about is the deep hunger in their bellies? A gospel that doesn't care for the poor, he says, is heresy.

But a gospel that is shared through the spiritual practice of feasting together, rich and poor? That is a gospel worthy of devotion, vulnerability, and abundant delight.

9

On Going

Sycamore Creek

"Go forth into all the world to love and serve the Lord"
read the plaques above all the doors of the church I attended while in middle school. This was the Great Commission. *Go*, I read every week as I went back out to my
routine.

My tender teenage heart knew that prompt would
somehow shape my future. In both high school and college I was convinced that I was called to live overseas.
At the age of eighteen, I spent a gap year living in West
Africa, a formative experience that expanded my understanding of the world and also my desire to work
with food. In order to process my adventure of living in
an international community, I returned to the United
States and began my college studies in cultural anthropology. As I began to study the function of culture in
helping humans make sense of the world, I itched to
escape from the ivory tower that explained but didn't
embody my understanding of that time. One look at

the vibrant fabrics hanging in my closet—a wardrobe that fit in my West African home but had no place in the United States—conjured up memories of the hot fried plantains my friend Esther would make, or the drums that accompanied our semiweekly worship. After I turned twenty-one, I crossed the Atlantic again, this time studying East African history, culture, and wildlife in Tanzania.

Part wanderlust and part humanitarian passion, these adventures satisfied me more than the pace of life back home. I longed to know God through the vibrancy of cultures around the globe. During my semester in Tanzania, I began to consider where I would move once I finished college. From the thatched roof *banda* where I slept, I trapped spiders and slapped at mosquitos while dreaming of ways I could return to this life of adventure after graduation.

Near the end of my semester abroad, a visiting lecturer joined us at our East African campus. She offered some advice that crept under my adventure-happy skin.

"God says to every one of us 'Go into all the world,'" she told us, reminding me of that plaque above my church door and the call that formed me in the early years of adulthood. "Too often we default to our comfortable place, believing that if we're meant to do something adventurous God will tell us to go." As I nodded smugly, she continued, "The assumption should be that

God calls us to go outside of our place of comfort, until God makes it clear we are to stay there."

I was willing to go back to the steamy port of Cotonou or the brisk mountains of Iringa, back to buying passion fruit and plantain chips from vendors on the side of the road, back to flipping chapati and squeezing lime over fresh papaya. I knew that commission backwards and forwards, and I had no concern that God would ever ask me to stay put.

But by the time I donned my cap and gown, I had discerned my next adventure: the attic bedroom of my parents' new home in suburban Massachusetts and half a decade more in those ivory towers I'd earlier itched to escape. Sitting behind a computer and digging deep into books is where God challenged me to encounter the complex beauty of creation. And it was rooted in my home country, in boring suburbia. There I discovered the beautiful difficulty of going forth while staying rooted.

It turns out God's call to *go* is much more humbling, and in fact more challenging, than an exotic adventure for Christ. It is a call to go outside of my home, outside of the places that buffer me from the pain of my neighbors, to mourn with those who are heartbroken and eat with those who are hungry. It is not a call to find adventure in Jesus's name but a call to love the place from which we came and to care for the needs of those who ache within it.

For those at Sycamore Creek Church, the call to go is not a reminder on a plaque above the door; it is the daily mission of an entire community. It is meeting weekly for worship in places outside the church walls, holding worship in the spaces where people already gather, at the times that they are available. It is going into the city of Lansing, Michigan, to meet the needs of neighbors in the places they already inhabit. And it is sitting around tables to hold church in a pub, worshipping God over burgers and beer.

When Sycamore Creek Church began their satellite services in the city of Lansing, they had no idea they were responding to a local restaurateur's prayer. With tears of joy Ron, the owner of a local diner, recalled its beginnings: "I prayed to God the church would come to me." Ron's commitment to the difficult task of running a family business left him unable to keep things afloat and still make it to church on Sunday morning. He'd been lamenting his lack of worship opportunities and praying for a change in circumstance. That's when Tom Arthur, the pastor of Sycamore Creek Church, approached him with a crazy idea. Would he be willing to keep the diner open late one evening a week in order to host church? It was a double answer to prayer: the chance to worship for Ron and his staff and a steady flow of business in the slowest hours of the week.

When Tom was invited to take a ministerial role at Sycamore Creek Church, a decade-old Methodist church-plant in Lansing, Michigan, he knew his task was a difficult one. Coming in as the second pastor of a church-plant is like tending a sprout that has just come out of the ground: still tender, but eager to burst forth with more life. The church had built up its Sunday morning constituency of young families, the expected demographic of a suburban church. Still, Tom wondered how he could reach out to those who didn't fit in the regular church crowd. What would happen, he thought, if, rather than pulling people into church, church went out to where the people already were?

Eager to test out his concept, Tom approached coffee shops and diners with his idea: Can I host church in your business? The idea faced varying levels of enthusiasm from business owners until Tom arrived at Grumpy's Diner where he met Ron, who had been unable to take Sunday mornings off from his small, family-run restaurant to attend church. Ron couldn't believe the opportunity to host church in his place of business. But it was there that Sycamore Creek launched their first remote concept, Church in a Diner, at Grumpy's Diner in the fall of 2012. The setting has changed a few times since that first service. Following Ron's retirement, Sycamore Creek tested out other locations before settling on Buddie's Grill, the location of their current service: Church in a Pub. From the beginning, Tom's idea was not to do anything radical or new, but simply to bring Sunday morning worship out of the walls of church on other nights of the week.

Worship in the pub doesn't flow quite like worship in the sanctuary. As Tom likes to say, the architecture influences the experience. Unlike in a traditional sanctuary, where a worship band can hush the congregation when it's time to begin, in the pub patrons and servers continue to move around and converse—finding a table, scouring the menu, placing orders. Eric, the worship leader, starts with a few songs, strategically preparing the group for worship in their less-than-traditional setting. He starts each week with a mainstream song, recognizable to guests who have never been in a church before. The sound seeps into the bar in front of the room where worship is held, luring in guests who simply came out for a round of drinks after work. Bright posters advertising the service line the front entry of the restaurant as well as the doors of the bathroom stalls. A few curious onlookers peek into the room from the comfort of their dinner tables while others take the plunge and find a seat inside.

Eric hosts music gigs in restaurants and bars around the city. He knows the crowd likely to stumble upon their backroom service. He knows how their joy and longing are met when they listen to a local musician. He knows the community and fellowship they desire in addition to their burgers and fries. Monday night worship at Church in a Pub is the ideal place for Eric to merge his love of music in both churches and pubs. He understands how the fellowship built at a bar or around the table forms people's expectations of music, and then he reorients their experience to one of worship as well.

After the music ends, the service flows just like the liturgy of Sunday morning, with one exception: a server wanders in and out of tables, taking orders and delivering food to hungry worshippers. While Tom preaches, Haley quietly checks in on each of her tables. "You're a new face to me!" she says to folks who haven't been to the church before. Her bubbly personality is contagious, soothing newcomers who might be confused about the worship at hand.

Who else gets welcomed into community when the church goes out from its building to eat together? That's something that growing friendships with the owners and servers like Haley have spurred Tom to explore. He's particularly intrigued by the logistics of Jesus's final supper in the upper room. "Who was serving Jesus and his disciples during the last supper?" Tom ponders. With cooks and servers deeply involved in the logistics of each Church in a Pub service, Tom can't help but wonder how these same figures might have played out two thousand years ago. "Those are silent and unspoken characters. But who prepared the food, who set the table, who cleaned up? I never even thought of these characters until I had restaurant servers walking around while I'm serving Communion."

For Tom these characters are just as vital to the act of worship as the music minister or the preacher. By watching the same folks serve hamburgers and soda alongside bread and wine, Tom realized the necessity of seeing all the people involved in the preparation of a service and of a meal.

Most of the folks drawn to Church in a Pub find typical liturgy off-putting. Many spent their early years in traditional churches and found the experience wanting. They long for fellowship, for a community that sees them and their particular needs, but they have not found this hunger satisfied in the pews of their local churches, where community life centers around family dynamics. The most prominent demographic represented by people who wander into Church in a Pub is single adults in their fifties and sixties. While the children's lessons and parents' groups of a traditional church might feel welcoming to some, they can be painfully off-putting for those in a different phase of life. Dining tables and chairs and the background hum of rock music, however, connote a different kind of belonging. When a church plants itself inside a restaurant, folks who feel out of place under the shadow of a steeple suddenly find themselves welcomed into the process of worship, where their hunger for communion is met in an unexpected way.

In the comfort of a space that these newcomers know, the message takes on new meaning. It connects with their lived experiences and offers something tangible, even tastable. It meets their needs for community built on love. The space creates the expectation for "talking, sharing, having nothing to be quiet about," says Tom. "If you need to get up and go to the bathroom or step outside, you go." It's a space where people know how to behave comfortably, and they don't feel restricted by unspoken rules about what is appropriate or not. They come mostly for fellowship and also for dinner, a seamless service the least of their concerns. "The messiness is part of doing worship on the edge of the 'mission field,'" says Tom. This messiness, which feels quite like a boisterous family dinner, offers a sense of belonging that is fertile ground for the seed of Christ's love to take root.

After the service ends, many worshippers order another round of drinks or dessert, lingering together afterwards to discuss a book or just talk. "The after party is just as important as the party," remarks Tom. Church carries on, deepening the roots of all in the crowd.

One challenge Tom noted early on was including elements from Bible studies or small group experiences in the service without watering down the sermon. The space begged for dialogue, to give the guests gathered an opportunity to respond or to push back against the sermon. At the same time, it was important to the worship model that regular attendees never became so close they closed themselves off to newcomers. Tom preaches just as he would on any other Sunday but incorporates five-minute discussion times throughout the sermon, providing opportunity for reflection and engagement as well. Sometimes this looks like pushback—a dynamic that rarely if ever occurs in a sanctuary setting. But it's a balm to those who fear church doesn't have room for their questions or concerns. And it's the natural response to worship that takes place around the dining room table.

Tom knows and loves his town of Lansing. He regularly drives around town observing the places that might be conducive to church, questioning where and how people already gather, and wondering how he might minister to them with the love of God. Whether on a soccer field, in a bowling alley, or around the tables of another diner, grill, or pub, Sycamore Creek challenges the assumption of the call to go into the world while remaining committed to the place where they are rooted. Their primary goal is not to grow or to seek adventure, but to think small—extending the care and compassion of Jesus to neighbors, one burger at a time.

10

On Transformation

Table of Mercy

Early one morning, before the sun had risen fully, I stood at my post next to the five-foot-tall Hobart mixer. Several pounds of butter whipped together with sugar, doubling in volume as the paddle spun around the bowl. I weighed out flour, salt, and baking powder before reaching over to grab the cornstarch, a mundane ingredient that I use most every day. Nothing was special about this morning, nothing spectacular about the container of cornstarch this day. And yet, as I scooped a tablespoon into the flour for my dough, it dawned on me how incredible it is that cooks can pull together pieces of so many plants in order to create a simple cookie.

Green shoots sprout from the ground, becoming corn, or wheat, or sugar cane. Their various parts get extracted, clarified, and put to use by the knowing hands of cooks and bakers. Starches, proteins, and fats are used to sweeten, to structure, to create a good chew. It's a tale as old as recorded time, this miraculous transformation of ingredients. The domestication of wheat and barley, its transformation into bread, and the founding of the world's first urban cultures are inextricably linked.[1]

Humankind is the only species that cooks—some scholars have gone so far as to say that cooking is what makes us human.[2] Through this process of cooking, living plants die at the hands of a flame, their starches and proteins caramelizing to bring out the fullness of their flavor. They undergo a transformation, with death bringing them into their fullest selves so they might bring life to others. Death is inescapable for those who eat.

"Eating is a daily reminder of creaturely mortality," says Norman Wirzba. "We eat to live, knowing that without food we will starve and die. But to eat we must also kill, realizing that without the deaths of others—microbes, insects, plants, and animals—we can have no food."[3]

Whenever we eat, the food we consume becomes a part of us. It dies on our behalf, but that death is not an act of finality—it's an act of transformation. The molecules we absorb become the very substance that makes up our body.[4] This death makes way for the deepest form of communion, incorporating another life into our own.

When a group of people takes part in cooking together, they too are transformed. Everyone brings the various aspects of their cultural identity and family history with them to the kitchen. From the knife habits adopted in watching Dad chop vegetables, to the tips and tricks passed down from Grandma, or the recipes important to one's cultural heritage, working alongside others compels cooks to reflect on the people they've observed in their culinary training. It provides a platform to tell stories, to share different types of knowledge, and to co-create something important. As the ingredients change, so do the people who pass their stories on in the process.

Making food "requires us to attend with our eyes, ears, noses, mouths, and hands and draws on the knowledge we hold in our bodies," says food scholar Jennifer Brady.[5] It is a way of sharing with others a knowledge embedded in our hands and on our tongues, of orienting our bodies toward learning from one another. It is an act of humility, together taking the life of plants, animals, and microbes and preparing them to nourish ourselves physically and communally.

As people who follow a resurrected God, Christians need not fear death. Death is not *the* end; instead, it is *an* end that always leads to a new beginning. It is another opportunity for transformation, a chance at new life. Likewise, the death of a church is not necessarily something to be avoided. Those who journeyed through the life of the church have been forever transformed, and the welcoming of death provides the space for something new.

Table of Mercy touched dozens of men and women in Austin, Texas. Throughout its two-year span, pastor Alex Raabe thought intentionally about the ways he could use the kitchen as a place to transform lives. He sought to foster a church centered on full-bodied sacramentality. "We say we come together at the Lord's Supper, at the table," Alex reminds those curious about his inspiration. "Well what does that look like if we spin it out into something much more obvious and tangible?" Some liturgical churches choose their decor with the intention that bigger signs connote larger meaning—a large baptismal font reminds of the importance of the sacrament, hefty loaves of bread signal the importance of its spiritual nutrition.

In keeping with this intention, Alex questioned what would happen if the Eucharist were taken to be something even bigger than a large loaf and a deep chalice—if it were taken to be a full dinner, cooked together as an act of worship. "All of our physical eating becomes spiritually nourishing, and our spiritual nourishing becomes physically fulfilling, even outside of church," he observes.

Just as a variety of ingredients work together to create the complexity of a good dish, Alex drew components of a variety of Christian traditions to develop the Table of Mercy service: the liturgy, a compilation of Lutheran, Episcopal, and Presbyterian traditions; the prayers, drawn from a variety of prayer books; the music, contemporary, juxtaposed with Orthodox icons for visual remembrance of the historical and global communion of worshippers. Every week the Bible readings were followed by a reading of poetry. Alex is convinced that God continues to speak through artists, particularly in Austin, Texas, a city full of creators. And so Alex incorporated art into every aspect of the Table of Mercy service.

From the start, Alex's primary goal for dinner church was to create a place that welcomed other folks like him—folks who did not fit in the mold of typical churchgoer, who might turn heads if they walked into a traditional church and might face cruel remarks if they engaged their doubts and concerns.

Every Sunday evening, Alex would invite worshippers to come cook together and prepare the space for worship. In the sunny kitchen of a local nonprofit, the group would chop, stir, and sauté together. Always using vegetarian and gluten-free ingredients, Alex ensured that no allergies or food aversions limited people's ability to feel welcome in the kitchen. The bustle of men and women cooking and chatting together provided a comfortable space for people to get to know one another. With bellies turned toward the counter and eyes glued to knife work, the vulnerability of getting to know new people didn't feel so charged. The process of whisking together a vinaigrette would compel the group to share stories of making salad at home with mom or harvesting lettuce in the garden with brothers.

Alex was approved to be a church-planter for the Lutheran church (ELCA) soon after finishing seminary. He completed an internship with Nadia Bolz-Weber at the House for All Sinners and Saints, an "incarnational, contemplative, irreverent, ancient/future church" dedicated to welcoming folks who seem to have nothing in common.[6] With Nadia's blessing, Alex aspired to create a community with a similarly welcoming feel in a town made up of folks that like to buck the trend. In the beginning, the church attracted primarily gay men, a demographic that felt wholly unwelcomed in most other church settings. It took a concerted effort on Alex's part to bring in women and straight people. "What church ever has that problem?" Alex chuckled as he described his beloved community. The church slowly built a strong community of about a dozen regular attendees, with new visitors dropping by each week. Though Alex faced pressure to build a church that attracted young adults, he knew that this was not the demographic group most in need of experiencing welcome into the church. Rather than focus on an age group, Alex focused his energy on those who considered themselves "post-church," who had grown up in a religious environment and found the experience wanting. Table of Mercy embodied God's hospitality and love and in turn proclaimed the beauty of Christianity as intimate and welcoming.

"Roughly one year prior to beginning to participate in Table of Mercy, I got hunted down by the Holy Spirit," says John, one such member. After growing up the gay son of Methodist pastors, John spent ten years away from the church, deeply scarred by rejection. "I began attending Table of Mercy loaded down with baggage, but desperately hopeful, and also desperately anxious about what this was going to be like."

As the components of the meal came together, worshippers would shift from kitchen to dining table. But before digging in to the feast they'd just composed, they opened with the liturgy of Communion. "God of our weary years, God of our silent tears, you have brought us this far along the way," they would pray. "In times of bitterness you did not abandon us, but guided us into the path of love and light. In every age you sent prophets to make known your loving will for all humanity. The cry of the poor has become your own cry; our hunger and thirst for justice is your own desire. In the fullness of time, you sent your chosen servant to preach good news to the afflicted, to break bread with the outcast and despised, and to ransom those in bondage to prejudice and sin."

Passing around a loaf of bread, some gluten-free crackers, wine, and juice—ensuring that no allergies or concerns limit access to God's table—they would share with one another a reminder of the death that makes way for new life. "We await the day when Jesus shall return to free all the earth from the bonds of slavery and death. Come, Lord Jesus! Send your Holy Spirit, our advocate, to fill the hearts of all who share this bread and cup with courage and wisdom to pursue love and justice in all the world."

The meal was served family-style, a true full-bodied communion of those made family in Christ. Conversation was never forced, which sometimes meant it would start and stop awkwardly. But the process of creating the space and the meal together, transforming an empty rented room into a sanctuary, drew the congregants together in such a way that silence was natural too. The process of getting to know one another as cooks, of working together in the same space, gave way to table conversation about the more mundane aspects of life, like names, and jobs, and hometowns.

Conversations ranged from social justice initiatives to favorite television shows to the food system in the city of Austin. Alex sees these times around the table as a beautiful reflection of the Kingdom of God, where art, pop culture, and pleasure became important topics of conversation in the midst of a holy and sacred space.

Physical eating provided spiritual nourishment, while the spiritual food made its way out into every aspect of life.

Only when the meal was finished and conversations had grown lively did Alex stand up to preach. Longing to provide space for worshippers to feel comfortable being vulnerable, Alex learned that he first must model such openness to his community. As a gay man, Alex cherished the ability to pastor a church where he need not "culturally commute," where he need not put on any personality apart from his own. This freedom afforded him the ability to be open and honest with his church about his own questions or concerns, inviting others to share their fears, their failures, their doubts, and their worries too. Like Alex, many of his congregants had been unwelcome in other churches, their own questions or doubts viewed as unacceptable in sacred spaces. At Table of Mercy they were freed from the burden of hiding behind others' expectations. "First-time visitors have shared things that are deeply personal and tragic," says Alex. When people experienced the vulnerability of a caring congregation, they knew that their own stories would be held tenderly by the community around them.

"The liturgical, sacramental, and communal space created a place where my spiritual scar tissue and wounds could be washed, cleaned, and allowed to slowly begin to heal," describes John. "While I couldn't say precisely when those scars became less visible or when those wounds had begun to close, at some point they did."

After two years, Alex was unable to continue renting the space that hosted the church. The primary grant that funded the church could not cover the rising rent costs in the city, and the district ultimately decided it was time for the church to close. When it came time to set the table for the last time, Alex did not fear the impending death. He and his members mourned and lamented—despite the promise of resurrection, death continues to sting. But they did not see the passing as a sign of failure. Rather, they viewed it as an opportunity for yet another transformation.

"These communities change the world even if they don't stick around forever," Alex said after his final service. "That's something church folks need to hear more about. Legacy doesn't just mean one-hundred-year-old buildings." Even a church that died in its infancy carries on through the legacy it left behind.

"Whether seen as a temporary way station or shelter, Table of Mercy embodied the meanings of sanctuary and refuge in the truest senses of the words for me," describes John. "I'm by no means without reservations, doubts, qualms, and baggage where Christianity and church are concerned. But I do now know that if it was possible to find such a faith community once, it's possible to find such a community again. To be able to look at Table of Mercy ending with a sense of gratitude and, dare I say it, hope for what the future holds, is nothing short of miraculous."

Though Table of Mercy might not meet in Austin anymore, those whose lives were transformed through their cooking with the worship community continue to nourish others. Alex now employs his pastoral skills while working in the kitchen at a local market, a company whose philosophy aligns with Table of Mercy's commitment to welcoming everyone to the table. He tells of coworkers who come to speak with him when they have no one else in their lives to whom they can turn. "I've been able to be a pastor to my colleagues, and that has been a lifesaver for me."

Yes, churches die. But look at those who have been transformed. Who would care about the green shoots sprouting from the ground if the time never came for a harvest? Who would care about the raw ingredients scattered about the cutting board if not for the heat of the flame transforming their flavors, making their goodness all the more powerful through death? It is only through death and the promise of resurrection that we move forward and nourish the world.

"Can a church be called a failure if it brings only one wandering, exhausted person to a place of rest, renewal, and belonging?" asks John. "If, as in the parable of the lost sheep, Jesus will wander far and wander wide in search of just one bewildered sheep and consider bringing that single sheep home a cause for celebration, I am living proof that Table of Mercy succeeded in its charism. Table of Mercy didn't simply bring me 'home.' It gave my home back to me."

Eating, cooking, and worshipping together are daily reminders of creaturely mortality. But death is not final—it is an act of transformation. In the words of the apostle John, when wheat dies it bears great fruit (John 12:24).

11

On Resurrection

Simple Church

After I opted to leave work in the restaurant industry, I spent a restless year questioning how God planned to fit together the circuitous journey I'd been on throughout my life. From as early as three years of age, I've suffered from debilitating anxiety brought on by slowness and silence. Throughout college and graduate school I experienced bellyaches and panic attacks whenever I found time to rest. As soon as I begin to feel comfortable in a place or a routine, a rush of worries floods my mind. I begin to fear my present path might limit my options in the future, and I fail to see the experiences and opportunities immediately before me.

During the year away from restaurant work, while exhausted by anxiety, I longed for clarity for the larger trajectory of my life. What I received instead was God's offer of peace through a passage in Fred Bahnson's book *Soil and Sacrament.* Telling of his own restless search for a life plan, a search that sounded frighteningly similar to my own, Bahnson describes the peace he found in the words of the prophet Isaiah: "When you turn to the right or when you turn to the left, your ears shall hear a word behind you saying, 'This is the way; walk in it'" (Isa. 30:21).

"For months I had agonized over what to do with my life, how I should live," he says. "When all along God had laid a path before me, inviting me to follow. I realized that all of my life I'd tried to wrestle free, to resist being taken, but this time—weary from the struggle—I simply allowed myself to be caught; I wanted to walk in the way."[1]

As I read through this chapter, the words spoke directly to me. *Follow the path that God has laid before you—allow yourself to get caught. Walk in the way.* As a constant reminder of this calling, I set a new background photo on my phone, a photo I'd taken in an apple orchard with a long, winding path speckled with the vibrant hues of Boston in the fall. Accompanying the photo was the text from Isaiah: *This is the way, walk in it.*

It turned out the way in which God intended for me to walk that year was back to the church where my research on dinner services all began.

The Simple Church community had launched my journey into the study of faith and eating, even if my acceptance of the simple lifestyle didn't come quite as naturally. So when Zach offered me a job at Simple Church, I accepted, but with hesitance. I was going to work only thirty hours per week, and, coming from the mad rush of restaurant work where sixty high-stress hours per week were my norm, I feared that so much free time would make me go crazy with boredom. I've never been good at staying still. But I had been observing the Simple community for several months, longing to learn what it meant to practice Sabbath, and ultimately an abundance of free time was precisely what I needed.

What I hadn't realized before stepping into the rhythms of simplicity, however, was that the calm I craved was not only about setting aside time just to be still. It also comes through setting aside anxious worries and desires for clarity and direction. My busyness was never just the result of a demanding job. It had been my way of masking my fear over lack of control. Slowing down might grant me the space to breathe, I realized, but I would need God to catch me in the silence of my newfound peace if I truly wished for change.

A typical week for the Simple Church staff looks quite different from that of a traditional church staff. We gather each morning over coffee and eggs—freshly laid by the chickens in the backyard—to pray through the daily liturgy of morning prayer. After discussing the day's Scripture readings and praying for every Simple Church participant by name, we split off to complete our various morning tasks. I spend most days in our Simple Bakeshop—a kitchen in the basement of the church space we rent. With the help of ministry interns and churchgoers, we mix, shape, and bake a hundred loaves of bread each week. Through the rhythmic process of kneading, we pray for one another and for all who will eat the bread our hands have made. Then we sit and enjoy a loaf, smothering it in butter or drizzling it with olive oil, balsamic vinegar, and a sprinkle of salt. It's a stark contrast to any bakery or restaurant I've worked in before, where I constantly factored how to piece together tasks so that not a second would go to waste. Like the tree-lined path on the background of my phone, each bite of a warm loaf draws me further into the freedom of this new life.

Simple Church sets up a tent at area farmers' markets to sell the bread and share the mission behind what we do. As shoppers wander by, we tell them about our church and invite them to visit on Thursday night. Many shoppers become regular attendees; some even ask for prayer in the midst of the busy market. Zach started selling bread just a few months after launching Simple Church in hopes of creating an extra revenue stream to take away pressure from internal giving. But as he continued to explore the deep spiritual parallels embedded in the process of baking, he realized that bread making itself was an act of worship.

In the first few weeks of working at Simple Church, I couldn't shake the guilt of slowing down my pace. While I valued the freedom from high-volume production, it felt irresponsible not to pack my days full of tasks and to-do lists. Our Simple staff doesn't avoid hard work, as evidenced by our burned and blistered hands striving for the callouses of seasoned farmers and bakers. Instead we pare down our day so that we can focus only on the most important tasks. To get the good of our work we simplify, focusing the church's finances, space, and time on things that bring our community to life. Once all that distracts is set aside, once delighting in God's creation becomes the central focus of a day, all of work becomes worship, rest, and play.

There are still moments when anxiety strikes. But often it is the rhythm of a Thursday service that puts my mind and body back at ease. God delighted in the entire process of creation, calling things good every step of the way. But I suspect the true joy came when God looked upon all of creation together in its beautiful interdependence and called it *very* good. While we strive to find the good in every aspect of work throughout the week, at Simple Church it is our Thursday worship, when the bread and soup and salad and community we've made come together at the table, that we experience true Sabbath. The supreme delight in feasting on bread and soup with the men and women whose lives have become intertwined with my own is slowly transforming my ability to delight in the mundane tasks of every other day. With every meal I grow more convinced that this is precisely how resurrection works, bringing us back to life as we rest and delight in the path God lays before us.

We gather on a Thursday night to eat. On another Thursday night, a long time ago, a group of friends gathered at a table together. And at that dinner, Jesus took the bread and he lifted it up and gave thanks. He broke it and gave it to his friends, saying, "Eat this in remembrance of me."

Every Thursday night, Pastor Zach opens the service at Simple Church with these words while lifting a seven-pound loaf of bread above his head. Giggles and shrieks of delight fill the room as he tears the loaf in half, the crackle of the crust and the rising steam evidence that it has just emerged from the oven. Ali and Lilly, two of the youngest Simple Church members, toddle around at Zach's feet with hands high in the air. Their eagerness to feast on the body of Christ spreads around the room.

Idealizing the experience of eating is easy at Simple Church, as though the idyllic setting provides automatic comfort. In reality, most folks feel a bit tense as they stand around the circle for the first time, exposed to an intimate crowd. Once plates have been served and guests are seated around the table, conversation often begins slowly. The discussion prompts are vulnerable; throughout the meal newcomers and old-timers alike confess their stories of regret and forgiveness. The intimacy and discomfort of Simple Church is no utopian ideal, yet despite the discomfort it somehow feels right. The tension built through vulnerable confession and intimate conversation around candlelit tables reflects the difficult questions and unknowns that come with following Christ. In this space, with everyone clutching their own mason jars of grape juice for safety, somehow the tension and confusion feel as though they are held by the presence of something greater.

After sharing only a few meals at Simple Church, one realizes that those committed to the church do not take these healing meals for granted. It was the slow decline of the North Grafton United Methodist Church and the inability to care for its building that prompted the start of Simple Church in the first place. Like many mainline Protestant churches in small New England towns, the Grafton congregation had dwindled down to a small handful of members. Rather than foot the costs of maintaining a large property, the church decided to close its doors. They sold the building in order to give the money, along with the parsonage—a three-bedroom house atop a hill with a working farm—to a young church-planter. As Zach neared his graduation from seminary, he was offered the Grafton location and the creative license to form a community he felt might best address the city's needs.

When Zach was an undergrad and then in seminary, he held Thursday night potlucks where deep theological discussion accompanied dinner late into the night. Thinking back on those days, Zach wanted to keep the dinner party going. "I always felt really excited and jazzed by those meetings. It was a buzzing excitement that I felt, and I always wondered why church couldn't feel more like that." Committed to a life of simplicity and a sense of a different way of gathering, Zach envisioned a community free from the stress of lots of events or fund-raising campaigns. He spent two months knocking on doors to get to know neighbors and tell them about his dinner-party-church idea before launching the first service in the basement of the parsonage. The group quickly outgrew that space, but rather than take on the costs and environmental impact of purchasing additional property, he opted to gather in the basement of another area church. In doing so, the impact is split between two communities, and neither building is left empty throughout the week.

As the church celebrates its third birthday, all members are poignantly aware that unless they actively seek the thriving of the community together, the death of another gathering is inevitable. But rather than lament the death of their former church or fear the possibility of death in their future, Simple Church focuses its attention on resurrection and on the sweet aroma of soup and bread providing respite through intergenerational community.

As Pastor Zach and his team tend life together on the parsonage farm, they watch God foster new life among the people who feast on the farm's bounty: Tim, a recent college graduate whose love for philosophy floods every conversation, gleans wisdom from Grace, a lifelong Catholic who has lived in the area for nearly seventy years. Lilly, a bright, red-headed three-year-old, engages Pastor Zach in important conversations about her love for music and for bread. Suzie, a thoughtful high school student, brings insightful commentary to table dialogue. Claire, a waitress and musician navigating early adulthood, values the ability to worship in a community that doesn't reject her for her sexuality. Mark brings his many questions and doubts—he's never been a part of any church before. The community gathers together to celebrate the finalization of adoptions. They pray weekly for Iris's daughter and Sally's grandchildren. They give rides to those who don't have cars or those who've had surgery and can't drive themselves. They bake cakes for one another's birthdays, especially when parents can't afford to provide the cakes themselves, and many gather together at Thanksgiving as well, especially when relatives live far away.

At Simple Church, members in their seventies are close friends with those in their twenties, middle schoolers genuinely love their pastors, and teenagers are considered wise enough to preach and speak. Everyone gleans from the wisdom of the church grandmas, the women who stuck with the community through the former church's death and Simple Church's resurrection. And even those who move away remain in close community with the friends they left behind.

The church has no Sunday school or membership course, no youth group or Christmas show, no microphones or robes—just six crimson tablecloths, a string of small white lightbulbs, a few sets of dishes, and a small playroom for the children to release their energy while the youth and adults converse. As a young church-plant, the community faces pressure from the denomination to continue growing in size. But Simple Church is not tied to the idea that large numbers are the hallmark of healthy community. Many participants fear that if their Thursday night meetings grow beyond forty guests a night, the community will cease to provide the respite and individual care that are central to the worship experience. Instead they hope to plant dinners in other neighborhoods on other nights, inviting more people to experience the value of a Simple Sabbath without risking the simplicity itself. Resurrection recognizes the fragility of all of life, sustained solely by the breath and direction of God. Growing numbers and steady streams of income mean little when not reliant on the God who holds each church, but small communities following the guidance of God can birth new life everywhere they turn.

Pastors and church-planters around the country lament the steady decline of churches. They diagnose the problem in a million different ways: secularized culture, lazy young people, poor theology, and on and on. But as Simple Church shows, the problem is not a lack of desire to worship or a lack of desire to experience God but a realization that worship is so much more than singing and praying and following a program inside a building on Sunday morning. When church is pared down to its simplest form, its rhythms encourage all who take part to set aside our own distractions. When the worship of our creative God is returned to the creation for which we give thanks, we find God's handiwork in the soil and the sky and a slice of freshly baked bread. We draw delight out of every detail of creation so that enjoyment becomes an act of worship. When church is simple, it ushers us out into the world, finding the evidence of resurrected life all around.

When we seek God in the mundane tasks of every day, anxiety over the larger trajectory of life is less all-consuming. Witnessing small signs of new life in all that God has made, the community at Simple Church and I remember that our job is simply to be caught by God's goodness. To listen to the still, small voice whispering in our ear: "This is the way, walk in it." No strategic planning or visioning meetings attempt to quell the fear that the wrong decision might limit any option of the future. There is just the process of slowing down, of simplifying, of standing, every Thursday, in a room full of people whose lives have become inextricably linked, like the flour and water and salt and yeast that nourish them week after week.

12

On Unity

One Holy Catholic and Apostolic Church

On that sticky summer Thursday during graduate school, the day my friends drove me out to my first dinner-church service, I witnessed the power of a meal to diffuse conflict. I participated, for the first time, in a conversation that sought to unify the Body of Christ through the sharing of bread. In this community, the phrase "one bread, one body" truly meant that the breaking of bread leads to the creation of a united community.

In the preface to Robert Farrar Capon's posthumous publication *More Theology & Less Heavy Cream*, David Zahl, director of Mockingbird Ministries, describes the ability of Capon's food writing to unite a broad audience. He says that an unabashed Christocentrism, a radically nonmoralistic approach to faith, a reverence for the elements, and obvious delight in all things kitchen-related drew in readers from a spectrum of backgrounds, Christians of a variety of traditions, and nonreligious folks alike. "Fr. Capon was also that rare scholar whose love of the Bible was truly contagious, a provocateur after God's own heart, unafraid to follow the Good News into every crevice of human experience," says Zahl.[1]

Capon wrote as though a high view of food inevitably accompanies a high view of Scripture, as though a high view of dinner parties inevitably accompanies a hunger for Communion, as though a high view of bread inevitably accompanies deep relationship with the Bread of Life. I am convinced, as Capon was, that in reverence for food and the ceremony around it, we will find the communion that God desires: evangelicals, mainline Protestants, and Catholics alike united over a truly contagious love of the Bible that leads us to follow the good news into every crevice of human experience—in the chew of a fresh sourdough loaf, the lingering scent of pepperoni, the crunch of potato chips, and the fellowship built around a table.

From the very beginning of creation, God commanded humanity to spread out, to fill the earth, to delight in the diversity of the world around them. When they failed to do so, the story of the Tower of Babel says God dispersed men and women, diversifying their language. God longs for a world full of varying languages and cultures that reflect the multifaceted nature of the Imago Dei, an image that can be grasped only when our diversity is understood and honored as a gift. We cannot fully know God outside of the many languages and cultures within the created world.

I've often heard this diversification of language explained as punishment, as though the Creator could be threatened by creation. However, in the story of Pentecost—the celebration that took place after Christ's ascension, when men and women all began speaking in languages not their own—we see what some label the reversal of Babel. Rather than reunify language into one, the Holy Spirit enabled people to speak and understand languages they had never heard before. Unity was created through the embrace of diversity, by recognizing that God is known more fully through the engagement of difference.

If language, a mode of communication based on what comes *out* of our mouths, reflects the multifaceted beauty of God, how much more can we know God by what we take *into* our mouths and incorporate into our very bodies? As anthropologist E. N. Anderson says, food functions as language.[2] The recipes and cuisines most dear to us—the food cultures that remind us of who we are and where we come from—allow us to know God more intimately. Through hospitality and sharing our love for food, we find the unity of Christ through the diversity of the body.

On Unity

For a year I traveled the country to attend each dinner church covered in this book. Though my own Christian journey has found me at home in a variety of denominations over the course of my life, some of the traditions I encountered this past year were completely new. Each church had a slightly different feel particular to its geographic context, its denominational affiliation, and the needs of the community in which it existed. Each had slightly different ideas about how to read Scripture, or what they believed Communion to be, or how they understood God's engagement with the world. They all used different terms to talk about their faith. I presume that readers may resonate deeply with some of these pastors, while the approach of others may seem troubling.

But what I discovered was this: every time I stepped into a new church, I thought back to the words of the Anglican priest as he ran into the elementary school gym where I worshipped at the time. *I was hit with the power of the fact that the Holy Spirit I so tangibly experience in our worship down the road is the exact same Holy Spirit here with you all as well.* The same Holy Spirit is present and active in every single dinner-church community.

At the time I first began my research at Simple Church, only a handful of other dinner churches existed. Slowly, I began to hear of more and more churches building on the concept. I began tracking each new church that emerged—managing a database that recorded the city, denomination, time of service, and website of each one. For a time, I thought I could manage to visit every dinner church in America. But over the course of three years, my database grew from five to more than fifty churches. Once the list hit fifty, I stopped keeping track, though I know the numbers continued to swell. It was clear that the Holy Spirit was at work in this growth. I needed to step back, close the database, and watch the Spirit move.

Could it be, I wondered, that this Holy Spirit longs to see the universal church recognize and value all that we hold in common more fervently than we do right now? Could it be that God is at work bringing us back to the table because our concerns should be more on living as, in the words of the Nicene Creed, "one holy catholic and apostolic church"?

In her book *Disunity in Christ*, Christena Cleveland shares a joke by comedian Emo Phillips to illustrate the depth to which small differences in thought divide Christians:

I was walking across a bridge one day and I saw a man standing on the edge about to jump off. So I ran over and said, "Stop! Don't do it!"

"Why shouldn't I?" he asked.

"Well, there's so much to live for."

"Like what?"

"Well, are you religious?"

He said yes.

I said, "Me too! Are you Christian or Buddhist?"

"Christian."

"Me too! Are you Catholic or Protestant?"

"Protestant."

"Me too! Are you Episcopalian or Baptist?"

"Baptist."

"Wow, me too! Are you Baptist Church of God or Baptist Church of the Lord?"

"Baptist Church of God!"

"Me too! Are you original Baptist Church of God, or are you Reformed Baptist Church of God?"

"Reformed Baptist Church of God!"

"Me too! Are you Reformed Baptist Church of God, reformation of 1879, or Reformed Baptist Church of God, reformation of 1915?"

He said, "Reformed Baptist Church of God, reformation of 1915!"

I said, "Die, heretic," and pushed him off.[3]

It's tempting to allow our differences to overpower all that we hold in common. While this example is meant to be both humorous and extreme, it takes only a quick glance through church history to see the ways in which differences in belief have led to fractures, some quite violent, dividing the body that is supposedly made one in

Christ. Differences in life experience, educational background, or theological influence lead to vastly different understandings of how to read Scripture and how to follow Christ. Even those who hold to the same holy text, the same sacraments of baptism and Communion—even those who hold to the same narrative of creation, death, resurrection, ascension, and restoration, the same belief that Christ has died, Christ is risen, and Christ will come again—find themselves so stifled by small differences that they cannot recognize their unity.

But Christ's vision for the church—the one that eats and drinks together in remembrance of his death and resurrection—is one in which no one part can say to the other, "I do not need you." It is inevitable that differences in language, culture, age, race, and life experience will cause people to understand God in differing ways and understand God's self-revelation through Scripture in differing ways. When this reality is viewed as an asset, as a vital aspect of how God desires to commune with us, we long to engage with those who think and live and believe differently than we do. And these engagements deepen our own understanding of who God is. But far too often, when we separate our intellect from our embodied engagement with the material world, we idolize right belief in the assumption that a single shared belief can and should exist to discourage divisions within the church.

But this dichotomy between belief and practice is impossible. "The way we inhabit the world is not primarily as thinkers, or even believers," says philosopher James K. A. Smith, "but as more affective, embodied creatures who make our way in the world more by feeling our way around."[4] God created us in culturally embedded human bodies such that our life experience always influences our understanding of who God is and how God engages with the world. We are, as Smith says, "the sorts of animals whose orientation to the world is shaped from the body up more than from the head down."[5]

So how do we bond despite our differences? We do so when we grasp and share the most basic need of all humanity: the need to eat and drink. We bond when we sit down at the table, claiming first and foremost that we eat and drink together in remembrance of Christ's death and resurrection, when we realize our ability to be unified as Christians even as we hold slight differences in belief. We form our minds through the practices of our bodies. Every time we sit in a pew or sit at a table, we train our minds to understand God and the world in particular ways. When we worship around a table with those who differ from us, we form ourselves into people who love the diversity of the Imago Dei and who crave the unity of Christ's body.

This embodied formation around the table allows for a variety of Christians to seek the unity that Christ calls us to; it also serves to welcome in those who do not feel comfortable stepping into a traditional church setting. Philosopher Lisa Heldke calls this kind of embodied formation "bodily knowledge."[6] Repetitive practices or rituals embed a certain kind of knowledge in our "gut"— a knowledge that goes beyond what we can cognitively understand or articulate.

Our bodies know, through our senses, how to sit at a table and eat. Those who grow up in a Catholic or Episcopal church know how and when to kneel or stand or sign the cross. Those who grow up in evangelical or Pentecostal churches might know instinctively when and how to worship through raised hands or closed eyes. This knowledge that our bodies hold forms not only our minds but also our feelings of comfort in particular places. Those who do not hold such knowledge of particular places feel their lack of belonging; they feel uncomfortable or perhaps even unsafe. For those who've grown up in church, the repetition of liturgy in a service of their own tradition can be a deeply meaningful way to worship. As an Anglican, I draw great sustenance from my Sunday worship. However, the rituals of the practice that I so love are exactly what can make those who've not grown up in the Anglican Church feel so out of place.

The knowledge of how to *do* church might seem natural to those who have grown up in it, which strengthens their feeling of belonging in Christian community. But for those who did not grow up in any particular type of church and did not develop a subconscious training in any particular form of worship, the rituals practiced by different kinds of communities only strengthen feelings of exclusion.

A dinner-church service draws people together through a form of bodily knowledge that is more accessible than the rituals of different church traditions—it draws people together through the knowledge of how to sit at a table and eat. It relies not on memory of the right chants to murmur but on a belly hungry for food and a heart hungry for community. It beckons all who thirst for companionship, for a space to ask questions, for healing from the pain of loneliness or rejection.

One member of Simple Church shared with me the depth of healing that took place when she began attending dinner services. She had grown up Methodist and understood how deeply the tradition grounded her life. At the same time, she saw her Methodist church as the root of much personal suffering and rejection for her sexual orientation. After leaving Christianity and exploring a variety of other religious and spiritual practices, she found that Simple Church allowed her to take baby steps back into Christian worship, allowing her to step back into the liturgies that formed her faith while also allowing her to address the pain more safely than a return to her former church would permit.

John, a member of Table of Mercy, explained his similar experience in returning to church. "The dinner-church model deconstructed 'church' enough for me to be willing to walk through its metaphorical door while simultaneously foregrounding the sacrament of the Eucharist. . . . If Table of Mercy did *not* reject me—if the people who came together to feed each other and, being gathered in the name of Jesus, thereby became Christ for each other through the celebration of the Eucharist—then I had an awful and wonderful problem on my hands. Wonderful—because it would mean reevaluating and rethinking my relationship to the religion I couldn't often stand or entirely quit despite my valiant effort to do so. Awful—because it would mean reevaluating and rethinking my relationship to the religion I could neither often stand nor entirely quit despite my valiant effort to do so. . . . I was being given the choice to accept the possibility of grace."

As powerful as the dinner-church model can be to unify the church, it would be naive to leave its limitations unacknowledged. Tensions around the sacrament of the Eucharist are very real. Among the questions raised by different traditions are these: Is the table meant to be open for all? Is it a way to encounter God on the tongue even before knowing the Lord in the mind? Is it meant to be a reconfirmation of baptism? Is it meant to be a ritual that unifies those within the church, binding us together in our shared belief? Can we consider this dinner-church communion the sacrament of body and blood, or must we call it something else?

Each pastor I've spoken with engages these questions differently. Some pastors choose not to serve bread or wine at dinner services in order to maintain the openness of the meal but preserve the closeness of the sacrament. Others choose not to serve bread or wine because they see the full meal as sacramental and don't think the specific elements are necessary. Some serve the bread and wine along with the meal, recognizing the entire meal as an outpouring of the Eucharist—their dinner-church theology formed through their open table theology. Others serve the bread and wine as bookends of the meal, their Eucharist theology opened up by their experience of dinner worship. By no means do I expect this dinner worship to resolve the disagreements between various traditions. However, I hope this book and dinner worship itself will create spaces to dialogue about the reason for and the implications of each practice and belief. What is clear is that God communes with creation through the process of eating, and the sharing of full meals is vital to the life of the church.

Another tension important to acknowledge is the racial dynamic of dinner-church worship as seen in this book and in the long history of full-meal communion in many church traditions. The pastors currently involved in the dinner-church dialogue are primarily, though not exclusively, white. I am aware that this is, in part, because of the way that I've chosen to define and limit my research of dinner churches. For the purposes of this book, I have chosen to look specifically at churches holding their services over the course of a meal, who consider the meal itself an act of worship.

At a recent food and faith conference, an African American woman asked me to describe a dinner church. When I called them churches that eat together as worship, she giggled and said, "Oh, honey. That's nothing special. That's all I've ever known as church!" The fellowship meal of African American and Caribbean American churches has long recognized the depth of connection between taking Communion and eating together as a church. They are not alone in connecting their food practices with theology.

Because humans are embodied creatures made in God's image and utterly dependent on food for survival, religion and cultural foodways have been deeply intertwined for every group of people throughout all of history. The myth that a pure belief transcending cultural influence is possible discourages recognition of this interdependence, particularly in white churches where the myth stakes its strongest claim. Outside of predominantly white communities, however, eating together at church has long been a valuable method of maintaining cultural identity and valuing the interdependence of cultural foodways and religious practice. For Pastor Tim Kim of Root and Branch, who was deeply formed by the weekly meals he shared growing up in a Korean American church, a great concern in leading a dinner church in Chicago is that his members will lose sight of the importance of meal-centered worship of communities that have come before them.

To laud the dinner-church model as something altogether new or as the ticket to fixing issues of diversity in the church only perpetuates the very ideas of white dominance that have pervaded the church, particularly the American church, for generations. In reality, most of the pastors whom I have spoken with recognize that their own churches are modeled after their observations of the power of food in communities of color. The dinner-church model is increasing in popularity among white communities because it recognizes the importance of embodiment and food in a way that white communities have historically devalued. This trend, then, is a valuable opportunity for white Christians to recognize the need to learn from traditions outside of our own. It is a valuable space for white Christians to recognize a desperate need for the meal-centered practices that others have long used. It's a way to recognize the power embedded in the process of eating together and the importance of Christ establishing his church around a meal. Even so, it is not the model that will inevitably heal the church's racial wounds. But perhaps it is a start toward recognizing that in one bread, we are one body.

I pray that this book will encourage white Christians to recognize all that we lose by not communing at tables set by Christians of color. I pray that this book launches further conversation about how eating as an act of worship can create the space for engaging difficult conversations. I pray that this book helps white Christians recognize all that we have to learn from communities of color who have long valued the role of the meal, and that it prompts us to question further what we can learn through these traditions about seeking racial healing in the church.

As theologian Claudio Carvalhaes says, "I believe that the Eucharistic table can hold the entire world around its borders and issue a call for justice and solidarity, salvation and liberation. As we open ourselves to our own and other's prayers, gestures, songs, movements, words and stories, and practices, we can and must create new worlds."[7] By eating together as Christ commanded, we take part in establishing God's vision for a new creation here today.

I pray that in all of our meals, no matter our theological, cultural, or ethnic backgrounds, we can meditate on the power of the meal handed down to us from Christ through generations and generations of his followers. I pray that we eat believing that, in the words of Sara Miles, this meal remains "through all the centuries more powerful than any attempts to manage it. It reconcile[s], if only for a minute, all of God's creation, revealing that, without exception, we [are] members of one body, God's body, in endless diversity. . . . At the Table, sharing food, we [are] brought into the ongoing work of making creation whole."[8]

Epilogue

I am asked all the time if I think the dinner church will become the new model of church and if I think that every worshipping community should become a dinner church. To be honest, my answer is no. I don't expect you to walk away from this book convinced that the only true way to do church is to follow the model of these communities. Even as I spend my days visiting and writing about meal-centered communities, my body still craves the high liturgical Anglican service I attend on Sunday mornings. I *do*, however, believe that every church and every Christian should understand the power of food and should expand their vision of what Jesus intended when asking his followers to eat and drink in remembrance of him. And I *do* believe these examples of worship around the table should inspire thoughtful reflection about who feels welcome or unwelcome in our churches, whom we see and whom we fail to see, who leaves lonely and who leaves grounded in community.

These churches should inspire all Christians to reflect on whether or not we really get the good, rest, and delight out of worshipping God, whether we understand the importance, power, and beauty of death, and whether we hold each example of resurrection with open hands before the Triune Lord, trusting that our churches and our lives belong solely to God.

Worship around the table is a communal search for every glimmer of goodness in an aching world. It's a communal search for resurrection. It is worship built on rest and delight and community. It is meeting the Creator at the table by communing with those made in God's image. This worship extends into every aspect of our living, setting us on a search for the ways that the Holy Spirit speaks in the places and through the people we otherwise don't see. This worship reorients our lives after the model of Jesus's self-sacrificial love. This worship inherently works against the personal and systemic sins that perpetuate the brokenness of the world, the "original sin" as Schmemann calls it, of ceasing to be hungry for God and God alone, ceasing to see our lives as dependent on "the whole world as a sacrament of communion with God."[1]

This worship takes place every time we sit down at a table with others to eat, whether we do so in a church, in a park, or in our tiny apartment dining room with a giant harp looming in the corner. God created us with two basic needs: to draw nutrition and energy from food, and to find companionship in sharing life with others. At the table, not only are these needs met, they can be met with great delight and joy as we commune with one another, with God, and with God's creation as well.

The gospel is a story of meals, a meal that brought destruction and a meal that brings life. God has used food as the driving force in the grand narrative of history, opening eyes to both goodness and evil in the act of eating. The process of growing, cooking, and eating mirrors the story of creation, death, and resurrection. When we eat, we take this story into ourselves. We proclaim with our bodies, our bellies, our whole lives, a trust in the Creator who is before and behind all things. We ground ourselves in the narrative of a God who created out of overflowing love, who aches over the brokenness of the world, and who is at work healing and restoring the beloved creation called good.

When Jesus established his church, he did so around the table. He asked his followers to eat together in remembrance of him, knowing that the process of sharing a meal communicates something vital about who we are and how we relate to God. When the church focuses on this practice of sharing the Eucharist together, allowing our identity as Christians to flow forth from the embodied practice of the faith, we bond over the shared need to eat and drink that is embedded in who we are as humans created in the image of God. Our embodied practices form us through communion with God and with one another.

It's of no small importance that Christ asked us to *do* something in remembrance of him. He didn't first ask us to believe in the right things but to practice them. We eat and drink, believing that Christ is present with us. We eat and drink, drawing near to God's beloved creation, believing that we are doing the work of establishing God's kingdom here on earth in the process. We eat and drink, understanding that our meals upset the divisions that keep us apart. We eat and drink, reversing that fateful bite that set us on the trajectory of death.

We eat together in remembrance of Jesus because it is at the table that we participate in the narrative God has been writing throughout all of history.

Something powerful happens at the table.

So go.

Feed Christ's sheep.

Acknowledgments

Many thanks to Zach Kerzee and all the folks at Simple Church. Thank you for being not just the subject of my research but also the community that embraced me, baked bread with me, and most of all, set a table for me. Thank you to Lindsay and Ashley for taking me out to my first dinner-church service.

To Emily Scott, Anna Woofenden, Bob Leopold and Mary Frances Beesorchard, Tim Kim and Neil Ellingson, Rachel Nance, Verlon and Melodee Fosner, Tom Arthur, and Alex Raabe, thank you for welcoming me into your churches and trusting me with your stories. Thank you for showing me a glimpse of the Spirit's movement at work through you.

Many thanks to the entire team at Eerdmans, especially to Lil Copan, for seeing the potential in my small little blog and encouraging me to write this book in the first place.

To Brian Howell, Christa Tooley, and Christine Folch, who encouraged my early fascination with the anthropology of food. To Nancy Ammerman and Norman Wirzba, who have guided my research on food and religion since.

To the entire food and faith community for cheering me on through the writing process, in particular to Nurya Love Parish for your commitment to creating connections and helping the Christian Food Movement grow.

To the churches that taught me to take joy in feasting, especially my dear community at Church of the Cross.

To Katherine, Renee, Katya, Tim, Claire, Emily, Julia, Megan, Spike, Robyn, and Rev. Stephanie, my wonderful models, photographers, and videographer.

To the ladies of Chez Heureuse: Gabrielle, Emily, and Heather. Thank you for creating a home that delighted in hospitality.

Hugs and tears and love to the Slack. Thank you all for being available around the clock for my anxieties and excitement, for reading and editing and reading some more. What a gift it is to write in community. I'm unbelievably grateful for each and every one of you.

Most of all, I am overwhelmed with love for the Vanderslice clan. Alyssa and Scott, Davis and Jessica, Emma Claire, and Isaiah, I'm not sure I would be so enamored with meals if not for all the laughter we've shared over dinner. Thank you, Mom and Dad, for setting a table every day that abounds in joy and forgiveness and that always has room to add another chair.

Notes

Introduction

1. Christena Cleveland, *Disunity in Christ* (Downers Grove, IL: InterVarsity Press, 2013), 75, 115, 149–50.

2. Larry M. Goodpaster, "Holy Communion and the Vision of the Beloved Community," in *Conflict and Communion: Reconciliation and Restorative Justice at Christ's Table*, ed. Thomas W. Porter (Nashville: Discipleship Resources, 2006), 41.

Chapter One

1. Norman Wirzba, *Food and Faith: A Theology of Eating* (Cambridge: Cambridge University Press, 2011), xii.

2. Alexander Schmemann, *For the Life of the World* (Crestwood, NY: St. Vladimir's Seminary Press, 1973), 16–18.

3. E. N. Anderson, *Everyone Eats*, 2nd ed. (New York: New York University Press, 2014), 83–84.

4. Jennifer Ayres, *Good Food: Grounded Practical Theology* (Waco, TX: Baylor University Press, 2013), 54–55.

5. Fred Bahnson and Norman Wirzba, *Making Peace with the Land: God's Call to Reconcile with Creation* (Downers Grove, IL: InterVarsity Press, 2012), 85.

6. Anderson, *Everyone Eats*, 171

7. Marvalene H. Hughes, "Soul, Black Women, and Food," in *Food

and Culture: A Reader, ed. Carole Counihan and Penny Van Esterik (New York: Routledge, 1997), 272–73.

8. Carolina Hinojosa-Cisneros, "On Theology, Food, and Storytelling," *Redbud Writers Guild* (August 1, 2017), https://www.redbudwriters guild.com/on-theology-food-and-storytelling/.

9. Sharon R. Sherman, "The Passover Seder: Ritual Dynamics, Foodways, and Family Folklore," in *Food in the USA*, ed. Carole Counihan (New York: Routledge, 2002), 195.

10. Sherman, "The Passover Seder," 201.

Chapter Two

1. Michael Symons, "Simmel's Gastronomic Sociology: An Overlooked Essay," *Food and Foodways* 8, no. 1 (1994).

2. Christine Pohl, *Making Room: Recovering Hospitality as a Christian Tradition* (Grand Rapids: Eerdmans, 1999), 5.

3. Michael Green, *Evangelism in the Early Church* (Eastbourne: Kingsway, 2003), 255–57.

4. Paul Bradshaw, ed., *The New Westminster Dictionary of Liturgy and Worship* (Louisville: Westminster John Knox Press, 2003), 136.

5. Meredith McGuire, *Lived Religion* (Oxford: Oxford University Press, 2008), 102–9.

6. Pohl, *Making Room*, 23, 54.

7. David Anderson Hooker, "Grandma's Supper Is the Lord's Supper," in *Conflict and Communion*, ed. Thomas Porter (Nashville: Discipleship Resources, 2006), 103–4.

8. Daniel Sack, *Whitebread Protestants* (New York: St. Martin's Press, 2000), 2.

Chapter Three

1. Norman Wirzba, "Food, Eating, and the Life of Faith," lecture, Duke Divinity School, Durham, NC, August 29, 2017.

2. Claude Fischler, "Commensality, Society, and Culture," *Social Science Information* 50 (August 2011): 533.

3. Claude Fischler, "Food, Self, and Identity," *Social Science Information* 27, no. 2 (June 1988): 282.

4. Robert S. Weiss, *Loneliness: The Experience of Emotional and Social Isolation* (Cambridge: MIT Press, 1973), 13, 20.

Chapter Four

1. Fred Bahnson, *Soil and Sacrament* (New York: Simon and Schuster, 2013), 179.

2. The names of all church members throughout the book have been changed for privacy.

Chapter Six

1. Wendell Berry, "The Solemn Boy," in *That Distant Land* (Washington, DC: Shoemaker Hoard, 2004), 182.

2. Norman Wirzba, *Food and Faith: A Theology of Eating* (Cambridge: Cambridge University Press, 2011), 46.

Chapter Eight

1. Robert Farrar Capon, *The Supper of the Lamb* (New York: Penguin Random House, 2002), 40.

2 Fr. Gregory Boyle. "Lessons from the Field: Kinship as an Intervention," lecture at College of the Holy Cross, Worcester, MA, February 6, 2017.

Chapter Ten

1. William Ruben, *Bread: A Global History*, Edible Series (London: Reaktion Books, 2011), 10–11.

2. Richard Wrangham, *Catching Fire: How Cooking Made Us Human* (Philadelphia: Basic Books, 2009).

3. Norman Wirzba, *Food and Faith: A Theology of Eating* (Cambridge: Cambridge University Press, 2011), 110–11.

4. Claude Fischler, "Food, Self, and Identity," *Social Science Information* 27, no. 2 (June 1988): 279.

5. Jennifer Brady, "Cooking as Inquiry: A Method to Stir Up Prevailing Ways of Knowing Food, Body, and Identity," *International Journal of Qualitative Methods* 10, no. 4 (November 2011): 326.

6. "House for All Sinners and Saints," accessed Oct. 11, 2017, http://houseforall.org/whoweare/.

Chapter Eleven

1. Fred Bahnson, *Soil and Sacrament* (New York: Simon and Schuster, 2013), 78.

Chapter Twelve

1. David Zahl, preface to *More Theology & Less Heavy Cream*, by Robert Farrar Capon (Charlottesville,VA: Mockingbird Ministries, 2016), xi.

2. E. N. Anderson, *Everyone Eats*, 2nd ed. (New York: New York University Press, 2014), 171.

3. Emo Phillips, "I Was Walking across a Bridge," in *Disunity in Christ*, by Christena Cleveland (Downers Grove: InterVarsity Press, 2013), 32.

4. James K. A. Smith, *Desiring the Kingdom: Worship, Worldview, and Cultural Formation* (Grand Rapids: Baker Academic, 2009), 47.

5. Smith, *Desiring the Kingdom*, 25.

6. Lisa Heldke, "Foodmaking as a Thoughtful Practice," in *Cooking, Eating, Thinking: Transformative Philosophies of Food*, ed. D. Curtin and L. Heldke (Bloomington: Indiana University Press, 1992), 204–29.

7. Claudio Carvalhaes, *Eucharist and Globalization: Redrawing the Borders of Eucharistic Hospitality* (Eugene, OR: Pickwick Publications, 2013), 14.

8. Sara Miles, *Take This Bread* (New York: Ballantine Books, 2008), 76–77.

Epilogue

1. Alexander Schmemann, *For the Life of the World* (Crestwood, NY: St. Vladimir's Seminary Press, 1973), 18.